Helping
Children Succeed

Books by Paul Tough

Whatever It Takes:
Geoffrey Canada's Quest to Change Harlem and America

How Children Succeed:
Grit, Curiosity, and the Hidden Power of Character

Helping Children Succeed:
What Works and Why

Helping Children Succeed

WHAT WORKS AND WHY

Paul Tough

HOUGHTON MIFFLIN HARCOURT
BOSTON • NEW YORK
2016

For information about permission to reproduce selections from this
book, write to trade.permissions@hmhco.com or to Permissions,
Houghton Mifflin Harcourt Publishing Company, 3 Park Avenue,
19th Floor, New York, New York 10016.

www.hmhco.com

Library of Congress Cataloging-in-Publication Data is available.
ISBN 978-0-544-93528-0

Book design by Dylan Rosal Greif

Printed in the United States of America
DOC 10 9 8 7 6 5 4 3 2 1

For Charles, who is just getting started

CONTENTS

Helping
Children Succeed

1. Adversity

In 2013, the United States reached an educational milestone. For the first time, a majority of the country's public school students — 51 percent of them, to be precise — fell below the federal government's threshold for being "low income," meaning they were eligible for a free or subsidized school lunch. This wasn't an overnight development; according to data compiled by the Southern Education Foundation, the percentage of American public school students who are low income has been rising steadily since the foundation started tracking the number in 1989. (Back then fewer than a third of students met the definition.) Passing the 50 percent mark may be a symbolic distinction, but as symbols go it is an important one. It means that the challenge of teaching low-income children can no longer be considered a side issue in American education. Helping poor kids succeed is now, by definition, the central mission of American public schools and, by extension, a central responsibility of the American public.

It is a responsibility we are failing to meet. According to statistics from the U.S. Department of Education, the gap in eighth-grade reading and math test scores between low-income students and their wealthier peers hasn't shrunk at all over the past 20 years. (The gap between poor and wealthier fourth-grade students narrowed during those two decades, but only by a tiny amount.) Meanwhile, the difference between the SAT scores of wealthy and poor high school seniors has actually increased over the past 30 years, from a 90-point gap (on an 800-point scale) in the 1980s to a 125-point gap today. The disparity in college-attainment rates between affluent and low-income students has also risen sharply. And these days, unless children from poor families get a college degree, their economic mobility is severely restricted: Young people who grow up in families in the lowest income quintile (with household income below about $21,500) and don't obtain a B.A. now have just a one in two chance of escaping that bottom economic bracket as adults.

These disparities are growing despite the fact that over the past two decades, closing the test-score gaps between affluent and poor children has been a central aim of national education policy, as embodied in President George W. Bush's No Child Left Behind law and President Barack Obama's Race to the Top program. These government efforts have been supported and supplemented by a constellation of nonprofit groups, often backed by philanthropists with deep pockets and an abiding commitment to addressing educational inequality. Along the way, certainly, those efforts have produced individual successes — schools and programs that make a genuine difference for some low-income students — but they have led to little or no improvement in the performance of low-income children as a whole.

The ongoing national discussion over how to close those gaps, and whether they even can be closed at all, has not been confined to policy makers and philanthropists. Educators across the country are intimately familiar with the struggles of children experiencing adversity, as are social workers, mentors, pediatricians, and parents. If you work with kids who are growing up in poverty or other adverse circumstances, you know that they can be difficult for teachers and other professionals to reach, hard to motivate, hard to calm down, hard to connect with. Many educators have been able to overcome these barriers (with some of their students, at least). But I've spoken with hundreds more in recent years who feel burned out by, even desperate over, the frustrations of their work.

Those of us who seek to overcome these educational disparities face many obstacles—some financial, some political, and some bureaucratic. But the first obstacle, I would argue, is conceptual: We don't yet entirely understand the mechanisms behind childhood adversity. What is it about growing up in poverty that leads to so many troubling outcomes? Or to put the question another way: What is it that growing up in affluence provides to children that growing up in poverty does not?

These are the questions that I have been trying to answer in my reporting for more than a decade. My first book, *Whatever It Takes,* took as its subject the work of Geoffrey Canada, the founder of the Harlem Children's Zone, and examined, among other topics, how neighborhoods affect children's outcomes, and particularly how the experience of living in a neighborhood of concentrated poverty constrains children's opportunities. My second book, *How Children Succeed,* considered the challenges of disadvantaged children through a different lens: the skills and capacities they develop (or don't develop) as they make their way through childhood.

The particular focus of *How Children Succeed* was the role that a group of factors often referred to as noncognitive or "soft" skills — qualities like perseverance, conscientiousness, self-control, and optimism — play in the challenges poor children face and the strategies that might help them succeed. These qualities, which are also sometimes called character strengths, have in recent years become a source of intensifying interest and growing optimism among those who study child development. Many people, myself included, now believe that they are critical tools for improving outcomes for low-income children.

Part of the evidence supporting this belief comes from neuroscience and pediatrics, where recent research shows that harsh or unstable environments can create biological changes in the growing brains and bodies of infants and children. Those changes impair the development of an important set of mental capacities that help children regulate their thoughts and feelings, and that impairment makes it difficult later on for them to process information and manage emotions in ways that allow them to succeed at school.

That neurobiological research is complemented by long-term psychological studies showing that children who exhibit certain noncognitive capacities (including self-control and conscientiousness) are more likely to experience a variety of improved outcomes in adulthood. The most thorough of these studies, which has tracked for decades 1,000 children born in Dunedin, New Zealand, in the early 1970s, showed that children with strong noncognitive capacities go on to complete more years of education and experience better health. They're also

less likely to be single parents, to run into problems with credit, or to wind up in jail.

Since my book was published, in the fall of 2012, the notion that these qualities are an important and often overlooked aspect of young people's development has continued to spread, especially within the education field. But for all the discussion of noncognitive factors in recent years, there has been little conclusive agreement on how best to help young people develop them. This has been understandably frustrating for many educators. After my book came out, I would sometimes speak before groups of teachers or child-development professionals. I'd talk about the latest research on the biology of adversity and describe the doctors and mentors and teachers and children I encountered in my reporting. And then, after telling my stories, I would often be met with the same question from the audience: *OK, now that we know this, what do we do?* The idea that noncognitive skills are an important element of educational success, especially among low-income students, resonated with the personal experience of many of the teachers I spoke to. But they hadn't seen, in my book or anywhere else, a clear description of which practices and approaches were most effective in developing those skills in children and adolescents.

And so, in the summer of 2014, I decided to embark on a new venture, revisiting the research that I wrote about in *How Children Succeed* and extending my reporting to new scientific discoveries, new school models, and new approaches to intervention with children, both inside and outside the classroom. This book is the culmination of that effort. It is intended to provide practitioners and policy makers with a practical guide to the research that makes up this nascent field. It is an attempt to answer the question: Now that we know this, what do we do?

2. Strategies

Before I begin, I want to briefly address a couple of strategies that I'll try to adhere to in the pages that follow. First, let me acknowledge a technique that journalists who write about social issues, as I do, often employ in our work. We describe a particular intervention — a school or a pedagogy or an after-school program or a community organization — and try to use that program, either explicitly or implicitly, as a model for others to emulate. Philanthropists and foundations that have as their mission improving the lives of the poor often do something similar: They look for programs that work and try to replicate them, scale them up to reach as broad an audience as possible. There are solid reasons behind the replication strategy. It is the basic growth paradigm of the technology world, in fact: Try a bunch of new things, identify the one that is most successful, and ramp it up. Focusing on successful models is an attractive approach for a narrative journalist, too, because people generally prefer reading emotionally resonant stories about individuals in pursuit of a

worthy goal to slogging through lots of dry research and statistics.

But there are limitations to this kind of journalism — and this kind of philanthropy, too. Scaling up doesn't work as well in social service and education as it does in the tech world. The social-science literature is rife with examples of small, high-quality programs that seem to become much less effective when they expand and replicate. And the focus on individual stories, while satisfying in a narrative sense, can also distract us from what is arguably a more significant question: If this school (or preschool or mentoring program) works, *why* does it work? What are the principles and practices that make it successful?

So my aim here is to examine interventions not as model programs to be replicated but as expressions of certain underlying ideas and strategies. My premise is that no program or school is perfect, but that each successful intervention contains some clues about how and why it works that can inform the rest of the field. My goal is to extract and explain the core principles of each program I write about and look for common threads running through them.

There is a second challenge facing anyone trying to find strategies to address the problems of disadvantaged children. In this country, at least, we tend to divide childhood into a series of discrete chapters, segmented like clothing sizes or the aisles in a public library: infants and toddlers over here, elementary school students over there, teenagers somewhere else entirely. This is broadly true of researchers, of advocacy groups, of philanthropies, and of government bureaucracies. Take public policy. On the federal level, children's education in their earliest years is the province of the Department of Health and Human Services, which runs Head Start and other early-childhood programs through its Administration for Children and Families. On the first day of kindergarten, though, responsibility for a child's education is magically whisked over to the Department of Education, which oversees primary and secondary education. This same bureaucratic divide occurs at the state and county level, where, with rare exceptions, early-childhood and school-system administrators do not collaborate or even communicate much.

These divisions are understandable. Trying to take on the full scope of childhood can seem too sprawling a mission for any one government agency or foundation, let alone any teacher or mentor or social worker. But the chief drawback to this fragmented approach is that we can miss the common themes and patterns that persist through the stages of a child's life. I aim here to follow a different strategy: to consider the developmental journey of children, and particularly children growing up in circumstances of adversity, as a continuum — a single unbroken story from birth through the end of high school.

* * *

3. Skills

Because noncognitive qualities like grit, curiosity, self-control, optimism, and conscientiousness are often described, with some accuracy, as *skills,* educators eager to develop these qualities in their students quite naturally tend to treat them like the skills that we already know how to teach: reading, calculating, analyzing, and so on. And as the value of noncognitive skills has become more widely acknowledged, demand has grown for a curriculum or a textbook or a teaching strategy to guide us in helping students develop these skills. If we can all agree on the most effective way to teach the Pythagorean theorem, can't we also agree on the best way to teach grit?

In practice, though, it hasn't been so simple. Some schools have developed comprehensive approaches to teaching character strengths, and in classrooms across the country, teachers are talking to their students more than ever about qualities like grit and perseverance. But in my reporting for *How Children Succeed,* I noticed a strange paradox: Many of the educators I encountered who seemed best able to engender noncognitive abilities in their students never said a word about these skills in the classroom.

Take Elizabeth Spiegel, the chess instructor I profiled at length in *How Children Succeed.* She teaches chess at Intermediate School 318, a traditional, non-magnet public school in Brooklyn

that enrolls mostly low-income students of color. As I described
in the book, she turned the I.S. 318 chess team into a competitive
powerhouse, one that regularly beats better-funded private-
school teams and wins national championships. It was clear
to me, watching her work, that she was teaching her students
something more than chess knowledge; she was also conveying
to them a sense of belonging and self-confidence and purpose.
And among the skills her students were mastering were many
that looked exactly like what other educators called character:
the students persisted at difficult tasks, overcoming great obstacles; they handled frustration and loss and failure with aplomb
and resilience; they devoted themselves to long-term goals that
often seemed impossibly distant.

And yet, in all the time I spent watching her teach, I never
once heard Elizabeth Spiegel use words like *grit* or *character*
or *self-control.* She talked to her students only about chess. She
didn't even really give them pep talks or motivational speeches.
Instead, her main pedagogical technique was to intensely analyze
their games with them, talking frankly and in detail about the
mistakes they had made, helping them see what they could have
done differently. Something in her careful and close attention to
her students' work changed not only their chess ability but also
their approach to life.

Or take Lanita Reed. She was one of the best teachers of
character I met — yet not only did she not talk much about
character, she wasn't even a teacher. She was a hairdresser who
owned her own salon, called Gifted Hanz, on the South Side of
Chicago, and she worked part-time as a mentor for a group called

Youth Advocate Programs, which had been hired by the Chicago schools department to provide intensive mentoring services to students who had been identified as being most at risk of committing or being a victim of gun violence. When I met Reed, she was working with a 17-year-old girl named Keitha Jones, whose childhood had been extremely difficult and painful and who expressed her frustration and anger by starting a fistfight, nearly every morning, with the first student at her high school who looked at her the wrong way.

Over the course of several months, Reed spent hours talking with Keitha—at her salon, at fast-food restaurants, at bowling alleys—listening to her troubles and giving her big-sisterly advice. Reed was a fantastic mentor, empathetic and kind but no softy. While she bonded and sympathized with Keitha over the ways Keitha had been mistreated, she also made sure Keitha understood that transforming her life was going to take a lot of hard work. With Reed's support, Keitha changed in exactly the way character-focused educators would hope: She became more persistent, more resilient, more optimistic, more self-controlled, more willing to forgo short-term gratification for a chance at long-term happiness. And it happened without any explicit talk about noncognitive skills or character strengths.

Though I observed this phenomenon during my reporting, it was only later, after the book was published, that I began to ask whether the teaching paradigm might be the wrong one to use when it comes to helping young people develop noncognitive strengths. Maybe you can't teach character the way you teach math. It seems axiomatic that you can't teach the quadratic equation without actually talking about the quadratic equation, and yet it was clear from my reporting that you could make students more self-controlled without ever talking to them about the virtue of self-control. It was also clear that certain pedagogical techniques that work well in math or history are ineffective when it comes to character strengths. No child ever learned curiosity by filling out curiosity worksheets; hearing lectures on perseverance doesn't seem to have much impact on the extent to which young people persevere.

This dawning understanding led me to some new questions: What if noncognitive capacities are categorically different than cognitive skills? What if they are not primarily the result of training and practice? And what if the process of developing them doesn't actually look anything like the process of learning stuff like reading and writing and math?

Rather than consider noncognitive capacities as skills to be taught, I came to conclude, it's more accurate and useful to look at them as products of a child's *environment*. There is certainly strong evidence that this is true in early childhood; we have in recent years learned a great deal about the effects that adverse environments have on children's early development. And there is growing evidence that even in middle and high school, children's noncognitive capacities are primarily a reflection of the environments in which they are embedded, including, centrally, their school environment.

This is big news for those of us who are trying to figure out how to help kids develop these abilities—and, more broadly, it's important news for those of us seeking to shrink class-based achievement gaps and provide broader avenues of opportunity for children growing up in adversity. If we want to improve a child's grit or resilience or self-control, it turns out that the place to begin is not with the child himself. What we need to change first, it seems, is his environment.

4. Stress

Which leads to a new and pressing question: Exactly what is it in the daily life of a disadvantaged child that most acutely hampers the development of the skills he needs to succeed? Part of the answer has to do with basic issues of health: Poor children, on average, eat less nutritious food than well-off children, and they get worse medical care. Another part of the answer has to do with early cognitive stimulation: Affluent parents typically provide more books and educational toys to their kids in early childhood; low-income parents are less likely to live in neighborhoods with good libraries and museums and other enrichment opportunities, and they're less likely to use a wide and varied vocabulary when speaking to their infants and children.

All these factors matter a great deal. And yet neuroscientists, psychologists, and other researchers have begun to focus on a new and different set of causes for the problems of children who grow up in adversity, and their research is recalibrating how we think about disadvantage and opportunity. These researchers have concluded that the primary mechanism through which children's environments affect their development is *stress*. Certain environmental factors, experienced over time, produce unhealthy and sustained levels of stress in children, and those stressors, to an extent far greater than we previously understood, undermine healthy development, both physiological and psychological.

Adversity, especially in early childhood, has a powerful effect on the development of the intricate stress-response network within each of us that links together the brain, the immune system, and the endocrine system (the glands that produce and release stress hormones, including cortisol). Especially in early childhood, this complex network is highly sensitive to environmental cues; it is constantly looking for signals from the environment to tell it what to expect in the days and years ahead. When those signals suggest that life is going to be hard, the network reacts by preparing for trouble: raising blood pressure, increasing the production of adrenaline, heightening vigilance.

In the short term, this may have benefits, especially in a dangerous environment: When your threat-detection system — sometimes referred to as your fight-or-flight response — is on high alert, you are always prepared for trouble, and you can react to it quickly. There are, in other words, some solid evolutionary reasons for these adaptations. But experienced over the longer term, these adaptations also cause an array of physiological problems: They tend to lead to a compromised immune system, metabolic shifts that contribute to weight gain, and, later in life, a variety of physical ailments, from asthma to heart disease. Even more ominously, stress can affect brain development. High levels of stress, especially in early childhood, hinder the development of a child's prefrontal cortex, the part of the brain that controls our subtlest and most complex intellectual functions, as well as our ability to regulate ourselves both emotionally and cognitively.

On an emotional level, chronic early stress—what many researchers now call toxic stress—can make it difficult for children to moderate their responses to disappointments and provocations. Small setbacks feel like crushing defeats; tiny slights turn into serious confrontations. In school, a highly sensitive stress-response system constantly on the lookout for threats can produce patterns of behavior that are self-defeating: fighting, talking back, acting up in class, and also, more subtly, going through each day perpetually wary of connection with peers and resistant to outreach from teachers and other adults.

On a cognitive level, growing up in a chaotic and unstable environment—and experiencing the chronic elevated stress that such an environment produces—disrupts the development of a set of skills, controlled by the prefrontal cortex, known as executive functions: higher-order mental abilities that some researchers compare to a team of air-traffic controllers overseeing the working of the brain. Executive functions, which include working memory, self-regulation, and cognitive flexibility, are the developmental building blocks—the neurological infrastructure—underpinning noncognitive abilities like resilience and perseverance. They are exceptionally helpful in navigating unfamiliar situations and processing new information, which is exactly what we ask children to do at school every day. When a child's executive functions aren't fully developed, those school days, with their complicated directions and constant distractions, become a never-ending exercise in frustration.

5. Parents

There is a paradox at the heart of much of the new research on early adversity and child development: While the problems that accompany poverty may be best understood on the molecular level, the solutions are not. These days it often feels as though you need a Ph.D. in neurochemistry to understand the full scope of what's going on in the lives of disadvantaged children. And yet the intricacies of that science — the precise mechanisms through which adrenal glands release glucocorticoids and immune cells send out cytokines — don't tell us much about how best to help children in trouble. Perhaps someday there will be neurochemical cures for these neurochemical imbalances — a shot or a pill that will magically counter the effects of childhood adversity. But for now, the best tool we have to correct or compensate for those effects is an unwieldy one: the environment in which children spend their days.

process known as methylation. Warm and responsive parenting when a baby rat is stressed-out—in particular, a soothing maternal behavior called licking and grooming—creates methylation effects on the precise segment of the baby rat's DNA that controls the way its hippocampus will process stress hormones in adulthood. And there are strong indications (though concrete evidence is still emerging) that the same methylation effects take place in human babies in response to corresponding human parenting behaviors. The McGill research validates what many parents (and former children, looking back on childhood) intuitively feel: Even small moments of parental attention can help nurture children's development on a very deep level—burrowing all the way down, it turns out, to our essential genetic code.

6. Trauma

But if home environments can have a positive impact on children's development, they can also do the opposite. We know that when children experience toxic stress, especially when they are very young, it can disrupt their development in profound ways, compromising their immune system, their executive functions, and their mental health. And while children are certainly affected by stressors outside the home, like neighborhood violence or abuse by a stranger, it is true that for a majority of children, the most significant threats to the development of their stress-response system come from inside their home.

One of the most important and influential studies of the long-term effects of childhood stress and trauma is the Adverse Childhood Experiences study, which was conducted in the 1990s by Robert Anda, a physician at the Centers for Disease Control and Prevention, and Vincent Felitti, the founder of the department of preventive medicine at Kaiser Permanente, the giant health-maintenance organization based in California. Together, Anda and Felitti surveyed a group of more than 17,000 Kaiser patients in Southern California—mostly white, middle-aged, and well-educated—about traumatic experiences they had undergone in childhood. The ten categories of trauma that Anda and Felitti asked patients about take place, in general, within the home and the family. These included three categories of abuse, two of neglect, and five related to growing up in a "seriously dysfunc-tional household": witnessing domestic violence, having divorced parents, or having family members who had been incarcerated or had mental illness or substance-abuse problems. In the survey, each respondent simply indicated how many different categories of adversity he or she had experienced as a child.

Anda and Felitti then dug through Kaiser's files for each patient's medical history. What they found was a startlingly strong correlation between the number of categories of trauma each patient had endured as a child and the likelihood that he or she had been afflicted by a variety of medical conditions as an adult. Patients who had experienced four or more adverse childhood experiences (or ACEs, as they came to be called) were twice as likely to have been diagnosed with cancer, twice as likely to have heart disease, twice as likely to have liver disease, and four times as likely to suffer from emphysema or chronic bronchitis.

Although the term *trauma* is often associated with isolated harrowing experiences, the categories that Anda and Felitti tracked were notable for being mostly chronic and ongoing. Children don't experience parental divorce or mental illness or neglect on a specific day; they experience them every day. What the ACE study was really tracking, more than adverse one-time *experiences*, was the influence of adverse *environments*. And that malign influence was shown to have a powerful impact not just on children's physical development but on their mental and psychological development as well: Anda and Felitti found that higher ACE scores correlated with higher rates of depression, anxiety, and suicide, as well as various self-destructive behaviors. Compared with people who had no history of ACEs, people with ACE scores of four or higher were twice as likely to smoke, seven times more likely to be alcoholics, and seven times more likely to have had sex before age 15.

More recently, researchers using Anda and Felitti's ACE scale have found that growing up in a chronically stressful home, as indicated by an elevated ACE score, has a direct negative effect on the development of children's executive functions and, by extension, on their ability to learn effectively in school. A study conducted by Nadine Burke Harris, a pediatrician and trauma researcher in San Francisco, found that just 3 percent of children with an ACE score of zero displayed learning or behavioral problems in school. But among children who had four or more ACEs, 51 percent had learning or behavioral problems. A separate national study published in 2014 (using a somewhat different definition of ACEs) found that school-aged children with two or more ACEs were eight times more likely than children with none to demonstrate behavioral problems and more than twice as likely to repeat a grade in school. According to this study, slightly more than half of all children have never experienced an adverse event, but the other half, the ones with at least one ACE, account for 85 percent of the behavioral problems that educators see in school.

7. Neglect

The large-scale disruptions in children's home environments reflected in the ten ACE categories clearly have detrimental effects on their development. But smaller family dysfunctions can have a negative impact, too. One recent study in Oregon looked at the effect that nonviolent arguments between parents had on infant development. The researchers took 6-to-12-month-old babies and, while they slept, scanned their brains with a functional magnetic resonance imaging, or fMRI, machine, which enables scientists to see which parts of a person's brain are being activated in response to different stimuli. While the babies were asleep, the researchers played recordings of angry-sounding nonsense speech. Separately, the infants' mothers filled out a survey about the child's home environment, including the frequency with which the parents argued. The result: Infants whose mothers had reported that there wasn't much arguing at home reacted relatively calmly to the angry sounds. But in infants whose mothers had reported that there was a lot of arguing at home, the fMRI showed flares of activity in regions of the brain associated with emotion, stress reactivity, and self-regulation.

This study and others like it help to show that there exists in children's lives a whole spectrum of environmental factors that fall short of the traditional definition of trauma but still have an adverse effect on brain development. In fact, a growing body of evidence suggests that one of the most serious threats to a child's healthy development is *neglect*—the mere absence of responsiveness from a parent or caregiver. When children are neglected, especially in infancy, their nervous systems experience it as a serious threat to their well-being; indeed, researchers have found that neglect can do more long-term harm to a child than physical abuse.

Neglect, too, exists on a continuum. Psychologists say that the mildest forms of neglect—occasional inattention from care-givers—can actually have a positive effect. It's good for children not always to be at the center of their parents' attention; to learn, at times, to engage and entertain themselves. At the other end of the spectrum is severe neglect, which by law constitutes maltreatment and necessitates intervention by child-welfare authorities. But in between those two extremes is a category called chronic understimulation, in which parents just don't interact very often with their children in an engaged, face-to-face, serve-and-return way, ignoring their cries or attempts at conversation, parking them in front of a screen for hours at a time.

Even this level of neglect, neuroscientists have found, has a profound and lasting disruptive effect on the development of the brain. Through its effects on the prefrontal cortex, neglect leads to impairment of the stress-response system, which in turn leads to emotional, behavioral, and social difficulties both in childhood and later in life. Children who have experienced chronic under-stimulation tend to engage in fewer social interactions with other children. They fall behind on measures of cognition and language development, and they have executive-function problems, too: They struggle with attention regulation; they are perceived by their teachers and parents as inattentive and hyperactive; they have trouble focusing in school.

According to neuroscientists who study the impact of stress on child development, the common thread among neglect, abuse, and other forms of trauma is that they communicate to the developing brains of infants and children that their environment is unstable, unpredictable, and chaotic. Especially in infancy, children's brains are looking for patterns in the world around them. And when their immediate environment is in constant flux — when the adults in their orbit behave erratically or don't interact with them much — the child's brain and the stress-response systems linked to it are triggered to prepare for a life of instability by being on constant alert, ready for anything.

But while it is true that behaviors like neglect and abuse can exert a disturbingly powerful influence on children, it is also true that the effect of some detrimental parental behaviors can be diminished or even reversed if those behaviors change. Consider, for instance, an experiment conducted in the 2000s in St. Petersburg, Russia, where the social and economic disruptions of the post-Soviet era resulted in many Russian infants being placed in orphanages. The institutions were far from Dickensian; children were given adequate food and clothing, a clean place to sleep, medical care, even toys. But they were run on a strict, impersonal model, and the staff never interacted with the children in a warm and responsive way. As one report described a typical Russian orphanage of that era, "Eating, changing, and bathing are typically done *to* the child mechanistically without the smiling, talking, and eye contact that would have been typical between a parent and a child in a family setting."

Then a team of Russian and American scientists trained the staff at one particular orphanage, where most children were under the age of two, in a new model of more sensitive caregiving. Staff members were encouraged to use everyday encounters like feeding and bathing as opportunities for warm and responsive interactions. Nothing big—just vocalizations and smiles, the kind of thing most parents do with their own children instinctively. Things changed for the orphans almost immediately. After nine months, they scored substantially better on measures of cognitive ability, social-emotional development, and motor skills. Perhaps most remarkably, the children improved physically as well. Though nothing changed in their diet or the medical care they received, their height, weight, and chest circumference (each of which had been stunted before the reforms) all measurably increased. And the caregivers benefited, too; they grew less depressed and anxious as the orphans they were caring for became healthier and happier. A relatively small change in caregiver behavior made a big difference in the lives of the children and in the emotional climate of the orphanage.

The St. Petersburg experiment worked because it changed the *environment* of the babies and children in the orphanage. And again, it is important to note that in the St. Petersburg orphanage, it wasn't the physical environment that changed. The children didn't get nicer beds or better food or more stimulating toys. What changed was the way the adults around them behaved toward them. If we want to try to improve the early lives of disadvantaged children today, there is considerable evidence that the best lever we can use is that same powerful environmental element: the behaviors and attitudes of the adults those children encounter every day.

8. Early Intervention

As I mentioned above, one of the premises I'm working from here is that childhood is a continuum, and if we want to help improve outcomes for disadvantaged children, we need to look for opportunities to intervene in positive ways at many different points along that continuum. Still, there is overwhelming evidence that early childhood—the years before a child's sixth birthday, and especially before her third—is a remarkable time of both opportunity and potential peril in a child's development. Children's brains in those early years are at their most malleable, more sensitive than at any other point to influences and cues from the surrounding environment. The neurological infrastructure is being formed that will support all of a child's future capacities, including not only her intellectual abilities—how to decipher and calculate and compare and infer—but also those emotional and psychological habits and abilities and mindsets that will enable her to negotiate life inside and outside school. The effect of the environment is amplified during the early years: When children are in a good environment, it is very good for their future development, and when they are in a bad environment, it is very bad.

The United States does not do a good job of reflecting this growing scientific understanding of early childhood, and especially early brain development, in its policies toward disadvantaged children. We dedicate only a small fraction of the public money we spend on children to the earliest years; in one recent international ranking, the United States placed 31st out of a group of 32 developed nations in the proportion of total public spending on social services that goes to early childhood. And what we do spend on early childhood goes mostly to prekindergarten, which generally means programs for four-year-olds (and a few three-year-olds) that are focused on academic skill building.

The data on the effectiveness of pre-K is somewhat mixed.

A growing number of statewide pre-K programs are universal, meaning that they are offered not only to disadvantaged children but also to children from better-off families. There are good political and social reasons behind making pre-K available to everyone, including the benefits to all children of socioeconomic integration and the fact that middle-class voters are more likely to be invested in programs that aren't narrowly targeted at the poor. But the educational value of pre-K for children who aren't poor is still in dispute; studies have found little or no positive effect (or even a negative effect) of universal pre-K programs on the skills of well-off children. That said, pre-K does seem to reliably help *disadvantaged* four-year-olds develop the skills they need for kindergarten, as long as the programs they are enrolled in are considered high-quality.

Still, the practice of devoting so much of our limited supply of early-childhood public dollars to pre-K means that we have very little left to spend on programs that support parents and children in the first three years of life. According to one estimate, only 6 percent of public early-childhood dollars in the United States go to programs for children who have not yet reached their third birthday. The remaining 94 percent go to programs for three-, four-, and five-year-olds. The problem with this lopsided division of resources is that we are now coming to understand with increasing clarity how much of the brain development that affects later success takes place in those first three years. The capacities that develop in the earliest years may be harder to measure on tests of kindergarten readiness than abilities like number and letter recognition, but they are precisely the skills, closely related to executive functions, that researchers have recently determined to be so valuable in kindergarten and beyond: the ability to focus on a single activity for an extended period, the ability to understand and follow directions, the ability to cope with disappointment and frustration, the ability to interact capably with other students.

The challenge for anyone who wants to help nurture the noncognitive abilities of low-income children in these early years is that the kind of deliberate practice children experience in pre-K doesn't do much to help develop their executive functions. Instead, those capacities are formed through their daily interactions with their environment, including, most centrally, the relationships they have with their parents and other adults in their lives. This leads to a dilemma for policy makers: The science tells us that parents and caregivers, and the environment they create for a child, are probably the most effective tool we have in early childhood for improving that child's future. But parental behavior, especially on the private, intimate level where baby talk and screen time and serve-and-return interactions dwell, is not something that most of us are entirely comfortable targeting with government interventions.

This dilemma is real, and solutions won't be easy to find. But in my recent reporting, I have encountered a number of organizations focused on enhancing the early-childhood environment — and especially what we might call the early-early-childhood environment, in the first three years of life. In the next three sections, I'm going to briefly describe a few of the most promising interventions they have developed. Some target parents;

others work to build supportive and nurturing environments outside the home. None is perfect, but together they may point the way to a new approach to intervening early in the lives of disadvantaged children.

9. Attachment

In 1986, in a few of the poorest neighborhoods in Kingston, Jamaica, a team of researchers from the University of the West Indies embarked on an experiment that over the past three decades has done a great deal to demonstrate the potential effectiveness of parent interventions. The experiment involved the families of 129 infants and toddlers who at the beginning of the study showed signs of delay in their development, either physically or mentally. The families were divided into four groups. One group received hour-long home visits once a week from a trained researcher who encouraged the parents to spend more time playing actively with their children: reading picture books, singing songs, playing peekaboo. A second group of children received a kilogram of a milk-based nutritional supplement each week. A third received both the supplement and the play-supporting home visits. And a fourth, a control group, received nothing.

The intervention itself ended after two years, but the

researchers have followed the children ever since. (They are now in their early thirties.) The result: the intervention that made a big difference in the children's lives wasn't the added nutrition; it was the encouragement to the parents to play. The children whose parents were counseled to play more with them did better, throughout childhood, on tests of IQ, aggressive behavior, and self-control. Today, as adults, they earn an average of 25 percent more per year than the subjects whose parents didn't receive home visits; by a variety of measures, including wages, these formerly delayed infants have now caught up with a comparison group of their peers who didn't show any signs of delay in infancy.

The Jamaica experiment makes a strong economic case for the potential effectiveness of some kind of home-visiting intervention with disadvantaged parents. But because the encouragement that the home visitors gave to parents was fairly general, the results don't necessarily tell us a whole lot about two important questions: Which kind of parental behaviors matter most, and which kind of direction or instruction from home visitors is most likely to incline disadvantaged parents to adopt those behaviors?

There is still considerable uncertainty within the field about the answers to those questions. These days there are three main approaches to home visiting in the United States. Sometimes they compete; sometimes they overlap. One group of interventions primarily targets children's health; another targets children's cognition, particularly their vocabulary and reading ability; and a third group targets children's relationships with their parents.

The most widespread home-visiting program in the country today is one that focuses primarily on health: the Nurse-Family

Partnership, which sends trained nurses into the homes of low-income expecting mothers, mostly unmarried teenagers. (There are currently more than 30,000 families enrolled in the program.) The nurses then visit the mothers regularly for the next two and a half years, counseling them about health-promoting behaviors, like quitting smoking, and offering advice on how to keep their children safe and how to get their own lives on track. The Nurse-Family Partnership has been studied in three separate randomized controlled trials, which have shown positive effects on the mothers, including reduced incidence of child abuse, arrest, and welfare enrollment. In most families, there was no significant impact of the home visits on the children's mental development or school outcomes, but in families where mothers scored especially low on measures of intelligence and mental health, children's academic performance did improve.

There is less solid evidence behind home-visiting interventions that target children's literacy and vocabulary skills. These interventions are premised on the real and pressing fact that children's early exposure to language, both spoken and written, varies widely by class. Well-off kids have on average more access to books and other printed materials; just as important, their parents speak to them more than low-income parents speak to their children—by some estimates, far more—and the speech they use is more complex. These trends correspond, at kindergarten entry, with a significant disadvantage on measures of vocabulary and language comprehension for low-income children.

Given this reality, many researchers and advocates have created experimental programs to try and narrow those gaps by encouraging low-income parents to read and talk more with their children. But it's hard to find reliable evidence that programs like these result in long-term improvements in the language abilities of disadvantaged children. The challenge is that infants absorb language from parents constantly, not just in dedicated teaching moments. So if you are a parent and you have a limited vocabulary, as many low-income parents do, it's not easy on your own to nurture in your children a rich vocabulary.

This is part of why many researchers now believe that the most promising approach to parental behavior change may be that third category: interventions that target the relationship between parents and children. Many interventions in this category are aimed at encouraging in children the development of a psychological phenomenon called parental attachment. In the 1950s, researchers in England, Canada, and the United States discovered that when infants experience warm, attentive parenting in the first 12 months of life, they often form a strong, attuned bond with their parents, which the researchers labeled secure attachment. This bond creates in the infants a deep-rooted sense of security and self-confidence—a secure base, in the researchers' terminology—that enables them to explore the world more independently and boldly as they get older. And that confidence and independence has practical, real-world implications: A landmark longitudinal study of attachment conducted at the University of Minnesota beginning in the 1970s found that infants who at age one showed evidence of secure attachment with their mother went on to be more attentive and engaged in preschool, more curious and resilient in middle school, and significantly more likely to graduate from high school.

Parents who are under a lot of stress, because of poverty or other destabilizing factors in their lives, are less likely than other parents to engage in the kind of calm, attentive, responsive interactions with their infants that promote secure attachment. But what excites many researchers today is the emerging understanding that those behaviors can be learned. It appears to be relatively easy to support and counsel disadvantaged parents in ways that make them much more likely to adopt an attachment-promoting approach to parenting. There's a chance, in fact, that certain successful parenting interventions promote attachment even when they are not trying to. It may be that part of what produces positive results in health-based interventions like the Nurse-Family Partnership, or read-with-your-kids programs, or even the Jamaican experiment, is that they involve home visitors urging parents to play and read and talk more with their infants — to engage in more serve-and-return moments, in other words — and those up-close parental interactions may have the effect of promoting secure attachment, even if attachment was not the intended target of the intervention.

So does this mean that if we want to promote secure attachment between stressed-out parents and stressed-out infants, the best approach is essentially informational: teaching parents the techniques and behaviors that are most likely to lead to a secure attachment? Can we just hand out some brochures to parents and produce more securely attached infants? Unfortunately, it doesn't appear to be quite that simple. It's certainly true that there are specific behaviors that help promote attachment — face-to-face play, a calm voice, serve-and-return interactions, smiles, warm touches. But for many parents, especially those who are living in conditions of adversity or who didn't receive a lot of attachment-promoting parenting themselves as kids (or both), the main obstacle to that kind of parenting is not that they haven't memorized the list of approved behaviors. It's that they are resentful and sleep-deprived and possibly depressed and don't feel much like serving and returning with the wailing infant in front of them who has a dirty diaper and a bad attitude about nap time. These stressed-out parents need more than just information. And, indeed, the most effective attachment-focused home-visiting interventions offer parents not just parenting tips but psychological and emotional support: The home visitors, through empathy and encouragement, literally make them feel better about their relationship with their infant and more secure in their identity as parents.

When interventions designed to encourage attachment are done right, the effect on disadvantaged parents and their children can be transformative. Another study conducted at the University of Minnesota included 137 families with a documented history of child maltreatment. These were parents, in other words, who had been found to have abused or neglected children in the past and now had a new baby to care for. The families were divided into a control group, which received the standard community services offered to families reported for maltreatment, and a treatment group, which instead received a year of therapeutic counseling focused on the relationship between parents and children. At the end of the year, only 2 percent of the children in the control group were securely attached, while 61 percent of the children in the treatment group were securely attached — a huge difference, and one that had enormous implications for the future happiness and success of those children.

10. Home Visiting

On a muggy day in July 2015, I spent the afternoon in St. Albans, a working-class neighborhood in Queens, New York, at the home of Stephanie King, the foster mother to Julianna, a sweet-natured girl just a few weeks shy of her second birthday, and her baby sister, Isabella. I was at Stephanie's house to observe a visit from Margarita Prensa, a parent coach with a home-visiting program called Attachment and Biobehavioral Catch-up, or ABC. The intervention, which is now used in the child-protection and foster-care systems at four sites in New York City, is the creation of Mary Dozier, a researcher in psychology at the University of Delaware, and it draws heavily on the principles of attachment psychology.

Like most children in foster care, Julianna was born into difficult circumstances. Her mother, a woman in her early twenties named Valerie, was living in New York City's shelter system when Julianna was born. About a month after Julianna's birth, Valerie sent Julianna to stay for the weekend with Stephanie and her partner, Canei, who were friends of Valerie's. When the weekend was over, Valerie announced that she couldn't take Julianna back. Instead of coming to pick her daughter up, she sent over a small bag containing all of Julianna's worldly possessions—some clothes and a couple of toys. Julianna has been in the custody of Stephanie and Canei ever since, though she still sees Valerie regularly, and Valerie is trying, eventually, to regain custody. A few months before my visit, Valerie gave birth to Isabella, her second child, and it wasn't long before Isabella was living with Stephanie and Canei, too.

These patterns of instability and uncertainty are exactly what make the foster-care process so damaging developmentally for so many children. And yet Julianna, during the time I spent with her, appeared to be doing just fine. And that, it seemed, had a lot to do with her relationship with Stephanie, an African-American woman in her early thirties with dyed red hair, an easy laugh, and a wry manner.

ABC uses home visits from coaches like Margarita to encourage parents and foster parents to connect more, and more sensitively, with the young children in their care. While we were visiting Stephanie and Julianna, Margarita kept up a steady stream of commentary as she watched the two of them interact: "You followed her lead nicely there." "Good delighting and smiling!" "She started crying, and you started rubbing her forehead. That's good; that's good nurturance." The goal of this narration is to make parents like Stephanie more conscious of the small interactions they are having with the children in their care. By drawing attention to and praising the moments that promote connection and attachment between parent and child, Margarita helped steer Stephanie toward better parenting approaches. And by accentuating the positive, rather than criticizing missteps, she underscored that good parenting is not rocket science—that Stephanie was, in fact, already performing many of these positive behaviors.

During much of our visit, Julianna was playing with a set of plastic stacking cups that Margarita had brought with her, the kind that come in a range of sizes so that each cup nests neatly inside the next-largest cup. At one point, as Stephanie and Margarita were talking about Isabella, Julianna started crumbling a cookie she was eating into one of the cups—and then suddenly threw a handful of cookie at Stephanie and her baby sister.

"No, Bobo," said Stephanie calmly, looking at Julianna. "We are not throwing cookies all over the place."

"Yes!" said Julianna. She stood a few feet away from Stephanie, staring at her, defiant in her white cotton pants and pink shirt.

Stephanie rose to her feet, still holding the baby. "Perhaps we're done with the cookies."

"No!" replied Julianna, her voice rising in pitch and volume.

"No, we're totally done with the cookies, because the cookie came over here to my part of the room." Stephanie reached down to retrieve the remaining cookie crumbs from Julianna's fist. "Give me that, please. Thank you very much."

Julianna started to wail. *"Nooooo!"*

Stephanie walked over to the garbage can in the kitchen to deposit the crumbs. "Can you sit down?"

"No!" But then Julianna did go and sit down. She said, sadly, "Oh no! No more cookies!" She looked down at her hands. "Cookies all gone."

"That's right, the cookies are all gone," Stephanie said.

Julianna stood up and started to cry. By this point, Stephanie was back in the living room. She kneeled down and handed Julianna one of the plastic stacking cups. "Have a seat," she said. "You can even have this. But we're done with the cookies."

Julianna sniffled a bit and then went back to playing with the cups.

"Are you OK?" Stephanie asked.

Julianna nodded her head.

They both looked at the big cup that Julianna was trying to fit into a smaller cup, with no success. "Can you get it in there?" Stephanie asked. "Here, let me show you."

Margarita, who had sat silently observing this whole interaction, now praised Stephanie's measured approach. "Good job," she said. "You stayed calm, and then you started following her lead right away." Stephanie smiled.

It was a small moment, but it was easy to see how the few minor choices Stephanie had made—keeping her voice low, redirecting Julianna's attention, being firm about rules but expressing sympathy for Julianna's feelings—had helped Julianna remain stable and relatively stress-free. And it was easy to see how different choices, the kind that might come more naturally to a beleaguered mom—taking Julianna's misbehavior personally, raising her voice, dwelling on punishment and retribution rather than moving on to a new moment—would have elevated Julianna's stress level, not only that afternoon, but over the long term.

When Dozier and other researchers have studied the impact of ABC on parents (including foster parents) and children, they have found consistently positive effects according to a number of indicators. One study found that after ten ABC home visits with foster parents, the children in their care showed significantly higher rates of secure attachment and were better able to regulate their behavior. Children's stress rates improved, too: Their daily patterns of rising and falling levels of cortisol, a key stress hormone, were no longer abnormal, as is often the case with children in the high-stress situation that is foster care. In fact, the cortisol patterns of the foster children of ABC-treated mothers are indistinguishable from those of typical, well-functioning, non-foster-care children.

A few weeks after my trip to Queens, I visited the Stress Neurobiology and Prevention lab at the University of Oregon in Eugene, where a team of researchers led by Phil Fisher, a psychologist, has developed a series of interventions with parents that in many ways parallel the ABC program, though with one major difference: They use digital video as a teaching tool to help steer parents away from behaviors that cause fear and stress in children and toward patterns that promote attachment and self-regulation.

The video-coaching program, which Fisher introduced in 2010, is called Filming Interactions to Nurture Development, or FIND. The basic strategy is similar to what Margarita Prensa was doing with the play-by-play narration she offered to Stephanie King—trying to draw a parent's attention to the small moments in parent-child interactions that are most beneficial for children.

With FIND, though, there is no coach narrating those moments in the present tense, the way Margarita did; instead, the videos help isolate such moments and, through careful review later on, render them especially vivid for parents.

Social-service agencies that use FIND usually employ teams of parent coaches who visit several at-risk parents or foster parents each day. When a FIND-trained coach arrives at a family's home, she sets up a video camera to record every inter-action between parent and child during the visit, which usually lasts just half an hour. In the evening, the day's videos are edited to highlight three brief moments that illustrate positive serve-and-return-style interactions. During the coach's next visit with that parent, she plays the video on a laptop or tablet, stopping it frequently to discuss with the parent why that particular interac-tion was meaningful and positive for the child.

The core idea behind FIND, Fisher explained to me, is that "serve-and-return is going on even in the most adverse home circumstances. Rather than get preoccupied in these homes with what parents are doing wrong, we just zero in on this one positive moment, and then we make the moment salient to parents by slowing things way down. The message to parents is: You don't need to learn something new. We just want to show you what you're already doing, because if you do more of that, it's going to be transformative for your baby."

* * *

11. Beyond the Home

ABC and FIND aim to improve outcomes for infants and children by altering their home environments in incremental but ultimately profound ways, slowly changing the basic tenor of their relationship with their parents. But other programs based on similar psychological principles seek to transform the environments where children spend time *outside* the home in their early years. The most intensive of these interventions is Educare, a network of early-childhood-education centers across the country that provide full-day childcare and preschool for children from low-income families, beginning as young as six weeks and continuing through age five.

Educare, which serves more than 3,000 children at its 21 centers, is intended primarily as a demonstration that even highly disadvantaged children can enter kindergarten ready to learn—but that in order to achieve that goal, they will need early interventions that are intensive (not to mention expensive). Right now, Educare costs about $20,000 per year per child—more or less the same as a year of public high school in a well-off suburb. (Educare families pay no tuition; an average of 16 percent of the funding comes from philanthropic support, and the rest comes from federal Head Start and Early Head Start funds and other government subsidies for low-income parents.)

In general, children in Educare live in high-poverty neighborhoods and in families with serious disadvantages, and children from those backgrounds are statistically more likely to be significantly behind their peers, by a broad range of measures, on the first day of kindergarten. Researchers have found, in fact, that most of the achievement gap between well-off and poor children opens up before age five; for most children, the gap then stays pretty steady from kindergarten through the end of high school. The premise behind Educare is that kids from disadvantaged backgrounds need two things in order to eliminate that gap: At age three and four, they need a high-quality preschool that provides them with a solid grounding in letters and numbers as well as a stable base of interpersonal, motivational, and psychological capacities. But first, before they set foot in preschool, they need to spend their first three years in an environment with plenty of responsive, warm, serve-and-return interaction with caring adults. And if they can't get that at home, they need to get it at a place like Educare.

The Educare centers I visited, in Tulsa, Chicago, and Omaha, were all beautifully designed and smoothly run, full of natural light and well-constructed play structures, and staffed by trained professionals. The Educare model puts as much emphasis on the development of children's noncognitive capacities as it does on their literacy and numeracy abilities, which means that kids in Educare centers are surrounded by lots of the interactive nurturance that fortifies their prefrontal cortex and leads to healthy executive-function development. The environment in the preschool classrooms I visited was invariably engaging and stimulating, yet still calm and warm. In the infant rooms, babies were being held and rocked, spoken and sung and read to. Even if conditions in the children's homes are chaotic and stressful, Educare's directors believe, the large dose of responsive care they experience each day at the center will allow them to transcend the potential ill effects of that instability.

Educare is currently conducting a long-term randomized controlled trial that, when it is completed in the next few years, may be able to conclusively demonstrate the program's effectiveness. But preliminary results already show powerful gap-closing effects for Educare students: If disadvantaged children enter Educare before their first birthday, they usually are, by the first day of kindergarten, essentially caught up with the national average on tests of basic knowledge and language comprehension, as well as on measures of noncognitive factors like attachment, initiative, and self-control. The economic case that Educare advocates make is that the savings that result from having those children caught up in kindergarten rather than lagging behind — savings down the road in special education, juvenile justice, and social services — more than offset the cost of Educare.

Because children spend so many hours each week at the Educare center, beginning at such an early age, the program has, more or less by default, a significant amount of control over their development up until their fifth birthday. And it may well prove to be true that children growing up in serious disadvantage require that kind of comprehensive, immersive intervention in order to catch up with their more advantaged peers. But there are other early-childhood experts who are testing out less intensive (and less expensive) interventions to see if it is possible to have an outsize effect on children's outcomes by altering certain critical elements in their daily environments in precisely targeted ways. One example: All Our Kin, which currently operates in three cities in Connecticut and reaches 1,500 children at a cost of less than $900 per child per year. All Our Kin achieves these efficiencies by focusing its energies on improving an environment that is almost always overlooked in discussions of early-childhood interventions: the informal, and often unlicensed, childcare providers with whom so many young children spend so much of their time, often in minimally stimulating or even dangerous conditions. All Our Kin does intensive community outreach to recruit these informal providers to enroll in the group's Family Child Care Network, where they receive, free of charge, regular professional-development training, plus biweekly visits from master educators who model high-quality childcare techniques for the providers and offer them long-term mentorship and guidance.

The help that the providers receive makes a difference in the care they give to the children they look after. Data shows that childcare sites in the network are significantly more conducive to children's development than other sites in the cities they serve. I visited two All Our Kin locations in New Haven, and while they weren't luxurious—both were in small, somewhat rundown homes in high-poverty neighborhoods—the childcare spaces were clean, bright, and organized, filled with books, art materials, and toys for make-believe play. The providers were engaged with and focused on the toddlers they were caring for (just five or six kids at each site) — always ready to offer support and redirection or just hugs when the children got frustrated or if minor conflicts broke out.

Another example of a high-leverage environmental intervention is the Chicago School Readiness Project, or CSRP, a professional-development program developed by Cybele Raver, a psychologist at New York University, that aims to enhance the self-regulatory abilities of children in low-income pre-K classrooms by making the school day less stressful for both teachers and students. Teachers in CSRP receive training in classroom-management techniques: how to set clear routines, how to redirect negative behavior, how to help students manage their feelings — all intended to provide students with a calm, consistent classroom experience. Mental-health professionals are also assigned to work in the classroom but are concerned as much with the mental health of the *teacher* as with that of the students.

Raver calls this approach "the bidirectional model of self-regulation." She believes that classroom climate is the result of a kind of feedback loop. When children whose self-regulatory abilities have been compromised by early toxic stress encounter the demands of a prekindergarten classroom, they often act out or otherwise misbehave. And when teachers are not trained in handling conflict or dealing with the disruptions that a child's poorly regulated stress-response system can produce, they often respond by escalating the conflict — which provokes a further escalation from the child. The classroom becomes a hostile, angry place. Children feel threatened, teachers feel frustrated and burned out, and behavior becomes the dominant issue for the entire school year.

But Raver contends that that feedback loop can function in the opposite way as well. If from the beginning of the year the classroom is stable and reliable, with clear rules, consistent discipline, and greater emphasis on recognizing good behavior than on punishing bad, students will be less likely to feel threatened and better able to regulate their less constructive impulses. That improved behavior, combined with the support and counsel of the mental-health professional assigned to the class, helps teachers stay calm and balanced in the face of the inevitable frustrations of teaching a group of high-energy four-year-olds.

The results of a recent randomized trial of CSRP showed that children who spent their prekindergarten year in a CSRP Head Start classroom had, at the end of the school year, substantially higher attention skills, greater impulse control, and better performance on executive-function tasks than did children in a control group. The children's improved self-regulatory capacity was evident both on the behavioral level—in their ability to sit quietly, follow directions, and maintain attention in the face of distractions—and on the cognitive level. The CSRP kids also had better vocabulary, letter-naming, and math skills, despite the fact that the training provided to teachers had included no academic content whatsoever. The students improved academically for the simple reason that they were able to concentrate on what was being taught, without their attention being swept away by conflicts and disagreements. Changing the environment in the classroom made it easier for them to learn.

12. Building Blocks

As I noted above, the first day of kindergarten is an important marker for our educational bureaucracies — that's the day, in most states, when "early childhood" officially comes to an end and the public becomes legally responsible for every child's education and skill development. And yet, in reality, nothing particularly consequential changes in a child's developmental journey on that first day of kindergarten. He is still the same kid, buffeted by the same social, environmental, and psychological forces that have guided his progress through his first five years. Children change, of course, as they grow. The executive-function abilities that are so critical in early childhood deepen and evolve into a more complex collection of habits, mindsets, and character strengths. But that growth happens throughout childhood, sometimes gradually, sometimes in sudden spurts, on a schedule that has little to do with the formal academic timetable.

Still, for most children the first day of kindergarten marks an important shift in the environment that influences and shapes their growth. From that day forward, most children spend more of their waking hours in the care of their teachers than in the care of their parents. This shift has two important implications. First, in a practical sense, it means that if we want to intervene in the environments of disadvantaged children, we will probably find more effective leverage, after age five, if we focus our attention on their school rather than their home. Second, developmentally, it means that children who have been growing up in adverse environments filled with stress now have a new arena in which those stresses can manifest themselves and multiply.

For children who grow up without significant experiences of adversity, the skill-development process leading up to kindergarten generally works the way it's supposed to: Calm, consistent, responsive interactions in infancy with parents and other caregivers create neural connections that lay the foundation for a healthy array of attention and concentration skills. Just as early stress sends signals to the developing nervous system to maintain constant vigilance and prepare for a lifetime of trouble, early warmth and responsiveness send the opposite message: You're safe. Life is going to be fine. Let down your guard; the people around you will protect you and provide for you. Be curious about the world; it's full of fascinating surprises. These signals trigger adaptations in children's brains that allow them to slow down and consider problems and decisions more carefully, to focus their attention for longer periods, and to more willingly trade immediate gratification for promises of long-term benefits.

Those abilities, even though we don't always think of them as academic in nature, are enormously helpful in achieving

academic success in kindergarten and beyond. And if you *don't*
have the mental tendencies that a stable, responsive early childhood tends to produce, the transition to kindergarten is likely
to be significantly more fraught, and the challenge of learning
the many things we ask kindergarten students to master can be
overwhelming. Which means that neurocognitive dysfunctions
can quickly become academic dysfunctions. Students don't learn
to read on time because it is harder for them to concentrate on
the words on the page. They don't learn the basics of number
sense because they are too distracted by the emotions and anxieties overloading their nervous systems. As academic material
becomes more complicated, they fall behind. As they fall behind,
they feel worse about themselves and worse about school. That
creates more stress, which often feeds into behavior problems,
which leads, in the classroom, to stigmatization and punishment,
which keeps their stress levels elevated, which makes it still
harder to concentrate—and so on, and so on, throughout
elementary school.

Perhaps because these emotional and psychological capacities have their roots in early childhood, many K-12 educators
assume that they are the responsibility of parents and early-childhood educators. Which means that when children arrive in
kindergarten without these foundational skills, there are often
few resources in place to help kids develop them, and school
administrators are often at a loss to know how to help.

Fast-forward a few years, to the moment when those students
arrive in middle or high school, and these executive-function

challenges are now, in the eyes of many teachers and administrators, seen as problems of "attitude" or motivation. But Jack Shonkoff, the director of Harvard's Center on the Developing Child, points out that that perception misses some important context. "If you haven't in your early years been growing up in an environment of responsive relationships that has buffered you from excessive stress activation, then if, in tenth-grade math class, you're not showing grit and motivation, it may not be a matter of you just not sucking it up enough," Shonkoff told me. "A lot of it has to do with problems of focusing attention, working memory, and cognitive flexibility. And you may not have developed those capacities because of what happened to you early on in your life."

A 2016 paper produced by a New York-based nonprofit called Turnaround for Children labeled these early capacities "building blocks for learning." According to the Turnaround paper, which was written by a consultant named Brooke Stafford-Brizard, high-level noncognitive skills like resilience, curiosity, and academic tenacity are very difficult for a child to obtain without first developing a foundation of executive functions, a capacity for self-awareness, and relationship skills. And those skills, in turn, stand atop an infrastructure of qualities built in the first years of life, qualities like secure attachment, the ability to manage stress, and self-regulation.

"When educators neither prioritize these skills and mindsets nor integrate them with academic development, students are left without tools for engagement or a language for learning," Stafford-Brizard writes. Without those skills, she adds, "they can't process the vast amount of instruction that comes their way each day, and it becomes daunting if not impossible to stay on track. This is the achievement gap."

The building-blocks model is, at present, mostly a theoretical framework, but it gives educators and anyone else concerned with child development a different and valuable lens through which to consider the problems of disadvantaged kids in the classroom. We want students in middle school and high school to be able to persevere, to be resilient, to be tenacious when faced with obstacles — but we don't often stop to consider the deep roots of those skills, the steps that every child must take, developmentally, to get there.

Over the course of the next few sections, I'm going to pull back from describing specific interventions and instead examine more deeply this process that Shonkoff and Stafford-Brizard describe. How exactly do the neurobiological adaptations that result from an adverse early childhood evolve into the social and academic struggles that so many disadvantaged students experience in school? How do most schools deal with those students? And what alternative approaches might produce better results?

* * *

13. Discipline

In her building-blocks paper, Stafford-Brizard writes that what children who have been exposed to significant adversity most need in school is "the opportunity to develop skills that may have been affected by their stress responses — meaning the ability to attach and bond, the ability to modulate stress, and most of all the ability to self-regulate." In reality, though, many schools and school systems look at students who are struggling in those areas and instead think: *How do we discipline them?* They don't see a child who hasn't yet developed a healthy set of self-regulation mechanisms; what they see is simply a kid with behavioral problems.

Our usual intuition when children and adolescents misbehave is to assume that they're doing so because they have rationally considered the consequences of their actions and calculated that the benefits of misbehavior outweigh the costs. And so our response is usually to try and increase the cost of misbehavior by ratcheting up the punishment they receive. But this only makes sense if a child's poor behavior is the product of a rational cost-benefit analysis. And, in fact, one of the chief insights that the neurobiological research provides is that the behavior of young people, especially young people who have experienced significant adversity, is often under the sway of emotional and psychological and hormonal forces within them that are far from rational.

This doesn't mean, of course, that teachers should excuse or ignore bad behavior in the classroom. But it does explain why harsh punishments so often prove ineffective over the long term in motivating troubled young people to succeed. And it suggests that school-discipline programs might be more effective if they were to focus less on imposing punishment and more on creating a classroom environment in which students who lack self-regulatory capacities can find the tools and context they need to develop them.

Most American schools today operate according to a philosophy of discipline that has its roots in the 1980s and 1990s, when a belief that schools would be safer and more effective if they allowed for "zero tolerance" of violence, drug use, and other misbehavior led to a sharp rise in school suspensions. This trend has persisted in much of the country. In 2010, more than a tenth of all public high school students nationwide were suspended at least once. And suspension rates are substantially higher among certain demographic groups. Nationally, African-American students are suspended three times as often as white students. In Chicago high schools (which happen to have particularly good and well-analyzed data on suspensions), 27 percent of students who live in the city's poorest neighborhoods received an out-of-school suspension during the 2013–14 school year, as did 30 percent of students with a reported personal history of abuse or neglect.

Sixty percent of Chicago's out-of-school suspensions are for infractions that don't involve violence or even a threat of violence: They are for "defiance of school staff, disruptive behaviors, and school rule violations." With the building-blocks model in mind, it's easy to see that kind of behavior—refusing to do what adults tell you to do, basically—as an expression not of a bad attitude or a defiant personality but of a poorly regulated stress-response system. Talking back and acting up in class are, at least in part, symptoms of a child's inability to control impulses, de-escalate confrontations, and manage anger and other strong feelings—the whole stew of self-regulation issues that can usually be traced to impaired executive-function development in early childhood. Given that neurobiological context, it's hard to argue that an out-of-school suspension will do much to improve that student's ability to self-regulate. What it *will* do, research suggests, is make it more likely that that student will struggle academically. And the students who are most likely to be suspended are already behind; in Chicago, high school students whose grades are in the lowest GPA quartile are four times more likely to be suspended than students whose grades are in the top quartile.

Advocates who make the case for suspensions often portray them as beneficial to the students left behind in the classroom, even if they're detrimental to the suspended students themselves. Get rid of the chronic trouble-makers, the argument goes, and the classroom will become calmer and more conducive to effective learning. But a 2014 study of nearly 17,000 students in a large urban district in Kentucky found the opposite. In those schools, a greater number of suspensions corresponded to lower end-of-semester math and reading scores for the students who were *never* suspended — even after correcting for various demographic indicators. Maybe a harsh disciplinary regime created more stress and anxiety for those kids in Kentucky than their disruptive classmates had. Or maybe teachers who didn't rely on suspensions as a default punishment were able to find other methods of calming down unruly students and restoring order and peace to a chaotic classroom. Whatever the cause, being in a classroom where your peers were likely to be suspended, even if you never got in trouble yourself, created an atmosphere that was less conducive to your academic success.

14. Incentives

The essential paradigm behind much of the school discipline practiced in the United States today — and certainly behind the zero-tolerance, suspension-heavy approach that has dominated since the 1990s — is behaviorism. The basic idea behind the behaviorist approach to education is that humans respond to incentives and reinforcement. If we get positive reinforcement for a certain behavior, we're more likely to do more of it; if we get negative reinforcement, we're more likely to do less. This paradigm is so dominant in American education that it often goes without saying. In most schools, the first few weeks of the school year are dedicated to discussions of class rules: incentives and disincentives, rewards and punishments, stickers and pizza parties, detentions and suspensions. And in many classrooms, that discussion continues more or less daily throughout the school year.

Clearly, on some level, behaviorism works. People, including children, respond well to behavioral cues, at least in the short term. But researchers are increasingly coming to understand that there are limits to the effectiveness of rewards and punishments in education, and that for young people whose neurological and psychological development has been shaped by intense stress, straightforward reward systems are often especially ineffective.

Roland Fryer, a celebrated young professor of economics at Harvard University, has spent the past decade testing out a variety of incentive schemes in experiments with public school students in Houston, New York, Chicago, and other American cities that have school systems with high poverty rates. Fryer has paid parents for attending parent-teacher conferences, students for reading books, and teachers for raising their students' test scores. He has given kids cell phones to inspire them to study harder. Altogether, he has handed out millions of dollars in rewards and prizes. As a body of work, Fryer's incentive studies have marked one of the biggest and most thorough educational experiments in American history.

And yet, in almost every case, the effect of Fryer's incentive programs has been zero. In New York City, between 2007 and 2010, Fryer oversaw and evaluated a program jointly administered by the city's education department and its teachers' union that distributed $75 million in cash incentives to teachers in some of the city's most low-performing schools. Fryer's conclusion after four years? "I find no evidence that teacher incentives increase student performance, attendance, or graduation, nor do I find any evidence that the incentives change student or teacher behavior. If anything, teacher incentives may decrease student achievement, especially in larger schools."

Between 2007 and 2009, Fryer distributed a total of $9.4 million in cash incentives to 27,000 students in Chicago, Dallas, and New York City, incentivizing book reading in Dallas, test scores in New York, and course grades in Chicago. Again, nothing. "The results from our incentive experiments are surprising," Fryer reported. "The impact of financial incentives on student achievement is statistically 0 in each city." Finally, in Houston in 2010–11, he gave cash incentives to fifth-grade students in 25 low-performing public schools, as well as to the parents and teachers of those students, with the intent of increasing the time they spent on math homework and improving their scores on standardized math tests. Although the students did perform the tasks necessary to get paid, their math test scores, at the end of seven months, hadn't changed at all, on average. And their reading scores actually went *down*.

In the Houston study, when there was some minimal improvement in test scores, it was only among the highest-achieving students, not the low achievers. A similar divide appears in other incentive studies as well. Jonathan Guryan, an economist at Northwestern University, conducted an experiment in which students were incentivized to read books over the summer, in the hopes of improving their reading comprehension. The more books students read that summer, the more money they received. Students did read a few more books in response to the incentives, but their comprehension scores on average did not budge. And as with the high achievers in Houston, in Guryan's study it was the students with the highest motivation who showed some (small) signs of improvement. The poorly motivated, recalcitrant students who were the real target of the intervention didn't benefit at all.

15. Motivation

So why don't incentives seem to work among the low-motivation, high-poverty students at whom they are often aimed? This is a big question, obviously, one that resonates well beyond the narrow issue of incentive programs. In fact, it takes us back to one of the central questions of this book: How do we motivate low-income children to work harder and persevere in school? Or, digging deeper: How do we motivate anybody to do anything? Economists, when they ponder that question, tend to reach a pretty straightforward conclusion: We motivate people by paying them or by offering some other material incentive. But economists aren't the only academics who address this subject.

Psychologists also spend their days contemplating the question of human motivation, and they often come up with answers that are significantly more nuanced than the default explanations of economists.

The stark fact that complicates incentive studies like Fryer's is that for children who grow up in difficult circumstances, there already exists a powerful set of material incentives to get a good education. Adults with a high school degree fare far better in life than adults without one. They not only earn more, on average, but they also have more stable families, better health, and less chance of being arrested or incarcerated. Those with college degrees similarly do much better, on average, than those without. Young people know this. And yet when it comes time to make any of the many crucial decisions that affect their likelihood of reaching those educational milestones, young people growing up in adversity often make choices that seem in flagrant opposition to their self-interest, rendering those goals more distant and difficult to attain.

Within the field of psychology, one important body of thought that helps to explain this apparent paradox is self-determination theory, which is the life's work of Edward Deci and Richard Ryan, two professors of psychology at the University of Rochester. Deci and Ryan came up with the beginnings of their theory in the 1970s, during a moment in the history of psychology when the field was mostly dominated by behaviorists, who believed that people's actions were governed solely by their motivation to fulfill basic biological needs and thus were highly responsive to straightforward rewards and punishments.

Deci and Ryan, by contrast, argued that we are mostly motivated not by the material consequences of our actions, but by the inherent enjoyment and meaning that those actions bring us, a phenomenon they labeled intrinsic motivation. They identified three key human needs—our need for competence, our need for autonomy, and our need for relatedness, meaning personal connection. And they contended that intrinsic motivation can be sustained only when we feel that those needs are being satisfied.

Deci and Ryan have, over the past few decades, conducted a series of experiments that together demonstrate that external rewards—the kind of material incentives that were at the heart of Fryer's studies—are not only often ineffective in motivating people to apply themselves to projects over the long term, but in many cases actually are counterproductive. In one famous early study recounted in Daniel Pink's book *Drive*, Deci, then a graduate student in psychology at Carnegie Mellon University, asked two groups of students to complete challenging puzzles. On the first day, neither group received rewards for their puzzle-solving ability. But on the second day, Deci told one of the groups that they would be paid $1 for each puzzle they completed. Then, on the third day, he told the group that was paid on day two that he'd run out of money, and so on that third day they would no longer be paid for the puzzles they completed.

Over the course of the three days, the group that was never paid grew gradually more engaged by the puzzles, simply because they were interesting and kind of fun, and each day they got a bit faster at completing them. When Deci secretly watched them through a two-way mirror, they kept working on the puzzles on their own time, trying to master them even though they weren't being timed or (they thought) observed.

But the group that was paid on day two but unpaid on day three exhibited different behavioral patterns. On the second day, predictably, they worked harder and faster, trying to earn their dollars. But on the third day, when Deci left the room, they mostly ignored the puzzles — they not only worked on them less than when they were being paid; they worked on them less than on the first day, when they had enjoyed the puzzles intrinsically, with no thought of payment. The introduction of rewards, in other words, had turned the exciting and stimulating game of puzzle solving into a job. And who wants to do a job if you're not getting paid?

Deci and Ryan and others have replicated this finding in studies with schoolchildren. In an experiment conducted by Mark Lepper, a Stanford psychologist, a group of preschoolers who liked to draw were told one day that they would get a reward — a blue ribbon and a certificate — at the end of the class for drawing some pictures. Two weeks later, they were noticeably *less* interested in drawing, and less likely to choose to draw during free time, than they were before the day of the experiment. Drawing had become for these once-eager four-year-olds a job, something worth doing only if there was a blue ribbon at the end.

In their writing on education, Deci and Ryan proceed from the principle that humans are natural learners and children are born creative and curious, "intrinsically motivated for the types of behaviors that foster learning and development." This idea is complicated, however, by the fact that part of learning anything, be it painting or programming or eighth-grade algebra, involves a lot of repetitive practice, and repetitive practice is usually pretty boring. Deci and Ryan acknowledge that many of the tasks that teachers ask students to complete each day are not inherently fun or satisfying; it is the rare student who feels a deep sense of intrinsic motivation when memorizing her multiplication tables.

It is at these moments that *extrinsic* motivation becomes important: when behaviors must be performed not for the inherent satisfaction of completing them, but for some separate outcome. Deci and Ryan say that when students can be encouraged to internalize those extrinsic motivations, the motivations become increasingly powerful. This is where the psychologists return to their three basic human needs: autonomy, competence, and relatedness. When teachers are able to create an environment that promotes those three feelings, they say, students exhibit much higher levels of motivation.

And how does a teacher create that kind of environment? Students experience autonomy in the classroom, Deci and Ryan explain, when their teachers "maximize a sense of choice and volitional engagement" while minimizing students' feelings of coercion and control. Students feel competent, they say, when their teachers give them tasks that they can succeed at but that aren't too easy—challenges just a bit beyond their current abilities. And they feel a sense of relatedness when they perceive that their teachers like and value and respect them. Those three feelings, according to Deci and Ryan, are a far more effective motivator for students than a deskful of gold stars and blue ribbons. If teachers want motivated students, they need to adjust their classroom environment and their relationships with their students in ways that enhance those three feelings. "Classroom contexts where students experience autonomy, competence, and relatedness tend not only to foster more intrinsic motivation," Deci and Ryan conclude, "but also more willing engagement in less interesting academic activities."

These motivational dynamics can play an even greater role in the school experience of low-income students, especially those whose development has been affected by early exposure to toxic stress. When children run into trouble in school, either academically or in the realm of behavior, most schools respond by imposing more control on them, not less, further diminishing their fragile sense of autonomy. As students fall behind their peers academically (as many low-income students do), they feel less and less competent. And when their relationship with their teacher is wary or even contentious, they are less likely to experience the kind of relatedness that Deci and Ryan have found to powerfully motivate young people. And once students reach that point of detachment and disengagement, no collection of material incentives or punishments is going to motivate them, at least not in a deep way or over the long term.

Yet schools that educate large numbers of children in poverty are generally run, even more than others, on principles of behaviorism rather than self-determination. These are often the schools where administrators feel the most pressure to show positive results on high-stakes standardized tests and where teachers feel the least confident in their (often unruly and underperforming) students' ability to deal responsibly with more autonomy. And so in these schools, where students are most in need of help internalizing extrinsic motivations, classroom environments often push them in the opposite direction: toward *more* external control, *fewer* feelings of competence, and *less* positive connection with teachers.

16. Assessment

When you read through Deci and Ryan's research on education, it quickly becomes evident that their discussion of motivational forces is very much connected to the conversations that educators have begun having about noncognitive capacities like self-control and grit. If we want students to act in ways that will maximize their future opportunities—to persevere through challenges, to delay gratification, to control their impulses—we need to consider what might motivate them to take those difficult steps.

Which brings me back to an idea I raised earlier: Perhaps we've been thinking about this new category of competencies all wrong. Maybe it's less useful to consider them as akin to academic skills that can be taught and measured and incentivized in predictable ways and more useful to think of them as being like psychological conditions—the product of a complex matrix of personal and environmental factors. And perhaps what students need more than anything for these positive academic habits to flourish is to spend as much time as possible in environments where they feel a sense of belonging, independence, and growth — or, to use some of the language of Deci and Ryan, where they experience relatedness, autonomy and competence.

So let's return for a moment to the ongoing debate over noncognitive skills and how (and whether) to define and measure them. You may recall that the original impetus for focusing on this previously unexplored set of skills, in *How Children Succeed* and elsewhere, was the growing body of evidence that, when it comes to long-term academic goals like high school graduation and college graduation, the test scores on which our current educational accountability system relies are clearly inadequate. Standardized-test scores are not irrelevant — students with high achievement-test scores do better, on average, in high school and in college than those with low scores — but those scores are not as predictive of success as other measures, including, most notably, GPA. A high school student's GPA, researchers have found, is a better predictor of her likelihood to graduate from college than her scores on standardized tests like the SAT and ACT. This is likely due to the fact that GPA captures more than just cognitive ability and content knowledge. It also reflects the noncognitive behaviors and mindsets and traits that enable students to leverage their existing cognitive skills more effectively in school.

What is frustrating to those who want reliable measures of these newly important skills is that it is quite difficult to isolate and define, using the blunt instrument that is a student's GPA, what exactly enables her to succeed. And in the current educational-policy environment—in which account-ability, based on empirical data, is valued so highly—if you can't clearly identify and measure skills, it's hard to convince people to take them seriously.

This has led to an active effort by educators, researchers, and policy makers to analyze and categorize noncognitive skills in the same way we would reading and math skills. Most of us agree that the SAT math section does a pretty good job of measuring a student's ability to do high school math (though there are quibbles, of course). But there is no similarly accepted measurement of a student's level of grit or conscientiousness or optimism. This hasn't stopped advocates from trying to develop those measures —and even to hold teachers and schools accountable for students' performance on them.

The stakes connected to these efforts are growing. In 2013, the U.S. Department of Education granted a waiver from the narrow test-based-accountability requirements of the No Child Left Behind law to a coalition of eight school systems in California, together named CORE (for California Office to Reform Education). In the spring of 2016, schools in these eight districts began using a new assessment system that includes a measurement, based on student self-reports, of students' growth mindset, self-efficacy, self-management, and social awareness. At the same time, officials around the nation have been trying to figure out how to respond to the new Every Student Succeeds Act, which replaced No Child Left Behind in December 2015 and requires each state to come up with its own accountability system that must include at least one nonacademic measure.

CORE is seen as one possible model for states to follow.

The challenge facing administrators is that student self-reports, which CORE uses, are by definition subjective, and if in the future a state decides to hold its teachers or principals accountable for their ability to develop students' noncognitive skills — if, say, next year's salary is dependent in part on increasing students' social awareness — there could be a temptation to influence or even manipulate the scores. In 2015, two leading researchers in the field of noncognitive skills, David Yeager of the University of Texas at Austin and Angela Duckworth of the University of Pennsylvania, published a paper investigating a wide variety of assessment tools for noncognitive skills. (Duckworth, as it happens, is the creator of the most widely used self-assessment measure for grit.) They concluded that when it comes to comparing students at one school or in one classroom with students in another, self-assessments just don't work — especially in cases where they are used as tools for accountability.

But there is another approach to evaluating these capacities in students that is worth considering — and it's one that might give us some new insights into the broader question of how to motivate struggling students to adopt more productive behaviors. A few years ago, a young economist at Northwestern University named Kirabo Jackson decided he wanted to investigate the ways we measure the effectiveness of teachers. He found a detailed database in North Carolina that tracked the performance of every single ninth-grade student in the state between 2005 and 2011 — a total of 464,502 students. The data followed their progress not only in ninth grade but through high school and beyond. Jackson had access to each student's scores on the statewide standardized test, and he used that as a rough measure of their cognitive ability. Then he did something new. He created a proxy measure for students' noncognitive ability, using just four pieces of existing administrative data: a student's attendance, suspensions, on-time grade progression, and overall GPA. Jackson's new index measured, in a fairly crude form, how engaged the student was in school — whether he showed up, whether he misbehaved, and how hard he worked in his classes.

Remarkably, Jackson found that this simple noncognitive proxy was a better predictor than a student's test scores of whether the student would attend college, a better predictor of adult wages, and a better predictor of future arrests. Jackson's proxy measure then allowed him to do some intriguing analysis of teachers' effectiveness. He subjected every ninth-grade English and algebra teacher in North Carolina to what economists call a value-added assessment. First he calculated whether and how being a student in a particular teacher's class affected that student's standardized-test score. This is the basic measure of value-added assessment in use today; teachers in many states across the country are evaluated (and sometimes compensated or fired) based on similar measures. But Jackson went one step further. He calculated the effect that teachers had on their students' noncognitive proxy measure: on their attendance, suspensions, timely progression from one grade to the next, and overall GPA.

What he found was that some teachers were reliably able to raise their students' standardized-test scores year after year.

These are the teachers, in every teacher-evaluation system that currently exists in this country, who are most valued and most rewarded. But Jackson also found that there was another distinct cohort of teachers who were reliably able to raise their students' performance on his noncognitive measure. If you were assigned to the class of a teacher in this cohort, you were more likely to show up to school, more likely to avoid suspension, more likely to move on to the next grade. And your overall GPA went up — not just your grades in that particular teacher's class, but your grades in your other classes, too.

Jackson found that these two groups of successful teachers did not necessarily overlap much; in every school, it seemed, there were certain teachers who were especially good at developing cognitive skills in their students and other teachers who excelled at developing noncognitive skills. But the teachers in the second cohort were not being rewarded for their success with their students — indeed, it seemed likely that no one but Kirabo Jackson even realized that they *were* successful. And yet those teachers, according to Jackson's calculations, were doing *more* to get those students to college and raise their future wages than were the much celebrated teachers who boosted students' test scores.

The most obvious thing we can learn from Jackson's study is that there are teachers out there making significant contributions to student success who are not being recognized by current accountability measures. What's more, those measures may be skewing teacher behavior in a way that is on the whole disadvantageous to students. If you're a teacher who is really good at raising noncognitive ability, but the teacher down the hall who is good at raising test scores is getting all the performance bonuses, you might be inspired to change your practices, despite the fact that you're already providing profound benefits to your students.

But beyond this important policy implication is a second implication in Jackson's study that is more relevant for our purposes: There is a more creative and potentially more useful way to measure noncognitive skills than what most researchers are currently focused on. Instead of laboring to come up with a perfectly calibrated new assessment tool for grit or self-control or self-efficacy, we can measure noncognitive capacities by measuring the positive outcomes that we know those capacities contribute to.

This conclusion then leads to an even deeper implication: It doesn't really matter if we label these qualities grit or self-control or tenacity or perseverance, or whether we define them as character strengths or noncognitive skills — or anything else, for that matter. For now, at least, it may be enough to know that for the students in Jackson's study, spending a few hours each week in close proximity to a certain kind of teacher changed *something* about their behavior. The environment those teachers created in the classroom somehow helped those students start making better decisions, and those decisions improved their lives in meaningful ways.

Because we tend to talk about school performance using the language of skills, we often default to the skill-development paradigm when considering these qualities: Teachers teach new noncognitive skills; students learn new noncognitive skills;

those new skills lead to different behaviors. And if that's the paradigm guiding our thinking, then of course we'd want to know exactly what those skills are, how to define them, how to measure them precisely, and how to teach them. What Jackson's study suggests is that what is going on in those classrooms may not really be about students acquiring skills, at least not in the traditional sense.

So here's a different paradigm, admittedly imprecise but, I would argue, a more accurate representation of what is happening in effective classrooms: Teachers create a certain climate, students behave differently in response to that climate, and those new behaviors lead to success. Did the students learn new skills that enabled them to behave differently? Maybe. Or maybe what we are choosing to call "skills" in this case is really just a new way of thinking about the world or about themselves—a set of attitudes or beliefs or mindsets that somehow unleash a new and potent way of behaving.

It's not hard to see some parallels here with the research on parenting that I wrote about earlier. Parent coaches in programs like ABC and FIND don't get hung up on which specific nursery rhymes and peekaboo techniques parents use with their infants; they know that what matters, in general, is warm, responsive, face-to-face, serve-and-return parenting, which can be delivered in many different flavors. That parenting approach, however it is carried out, conveys to infants some deep, even transcendent messages about belonging, security, stability, and their place in the world. And those mushy, sentimental notions find their articulation in the infants' brains in precise neurochemical reactions: the formation of a synapse, the pruning of a dendrite, the methylation of a DNA sequence. All of which contribute, directly or indirectly, to that child's future success in school.

The chain reactions taking place in the classroom may in fact be quite similar. Teachers convey to their students deep messages — often implicitly or even subliminally — about belonging, connection, ability, and opportunity. Those messages may not have the same measurable neurochemical effects on a ten-year-old brain as they do on a ten-month-old brain, but they do have a profound impact on students' psychology and thus on their behavior. When kids feel a sense of belonging at school, when they receive the right kind of messages from an adult who believes they can succeed and who is attending to them with some degree of compassion and respect, they are then more likely to show up to class, to persevere longer at difficult tasks, and to deal more resiliently with the countless small-scale setbacks and frustrations that make up the typical student's school day. In the same way that responsive parenting in early childhood creates a kind of mental space where a child's first tentative steps toward intellectual learning can take place, so do the right kind of messages from teachers in school create a mental space that allows a student to engage in more advanced and demanding academic learning.

* * *

17. Messages

So what are those messages? And how does a teacher convey them to students? This is a particularly lively question in education right now, and one of the most important scholars investigating the subject is Camille Farrington, of the Consortium on Chicago School Research. A former inner-city high school teacher, Farrington left the classroom after 15 years to get a Ph.D. in urban-education policy from the University of Illinois at Chicago. Like many high school teachers, she felt mystified by the behavior and choices that some of her students made. Why weren't they more consistently motivated to work hard and thus reap the benefits of a good education? Why did their motivation seem to ebb and flow in unpredictable ways?

When she began her doctoral studies in 2006, Farrington plunged into the latest research on the psychology of motivation. She read Deci and Ryan's work on rewards and incentives. She read Carol Dweck, the Stanford psychologist who discovered that students' motivation can be boosted or undercut by the messages they hear about their own ability to improve their intelligence. She read Daphna Oyserman, a multidisciplinary researcher at the University of Southern California who found that a student's level of motivation is highly dependent on her sense of her own identity as a student. At the same time that she was ingesting all this psychological research about motivation, Farrington was also studying the related sociological literature, which was concerned with how institutional structures affect individual behavior and, specifically, how certain educational structures—like school funding mechanisms, teacher contracts, or patterns of segregation—might incline students toward success or failure.

Farrington's research background, plus her history as a teacher in high-poverty neighborhoods, helped her think differently about what happens to students when they're at school. "I think I was predisposed to be thinking about environments," Farrington told me. She was particularly interested in what she called the "narrative" that exists within each school with regard to success and failure—the messages, subtle and not so subtle, that students receive when they fail. Moments of failure, Farrington believed, are the time when students are most susceptible to messages, both positive and negative, about their potential. If they hear the message that a failure is a final verdict on their ability, they may well give up and pull back from school. But if instead they get the message that a failure is a temporary stumble, or even a valuable opportunity to learn and improve, then that setback is more likely to propel them to invest more of themselves in their education. Farrington believed that these narratives about failure were especially resonant among students from low-income families, who were more likely to be anxious or insecure about the possibility of failing in an academic context.

In 2011, Farrington and a team of researchers at the consortium began a comprehensive review of the literature on noncognitive capacities and the role they play in educational success. The result was a report titled "Teaching Adolescents to Become Learners," published in June 2012, which for the first time represented noncognitive skills — or "noncognitive factors," as the report called them — not as a set of discrete *abilities* that individual children might somehow master (or fail to master), but as a collection of mindsets and habits and attitudes that are highly dependent on the *context* in which children are learning.

Within a field that was, at the time, mostly debating what grit is, how to measure it as a skill, which students possess it, and how it can best be taught, this was a novel approach. "There is little evidence that working directly on changing students' grit or perseverance would be an effective lever for improving their academic performance," Farrington and her colleagues wrote. "While some students are more likely to persist in tasks or exhibit self-discipline than others, *all* students are more likely to demonstrate perseverance if the school or classroom context helps them develop positive mindsets and effective learning strategies."

And what were those perseverance-friendly school or classroom contexts? To answer that question, Farrington realized that she needed to go back and essentially deconstruct the learning process, to pull from the existing research some basic facts about what students need to succeed and then build up a framework from there.

She started with some universally acknowledged positive academic outcomes for students: getting good grades, graduating from high school, and earning a college degree. What led most directly to those outcomes, she concluded, were *academic behaviors* like completing class assignments, coming to class

prepared, participating in class discussions, and, most fundamentally, showing up to school. So far, pretty straightforward, right?
Most teachers would agree that students who attend school and
do their homework and participate in class are more likely to do
well. The more urgent question is: What produces those positive
academic behaviors?

Farrington's answer was a quality she called *academic
perseverance* — the tendency to maintain productive academic
behaviors over time. What distinguishes students with academic
perseverance, Farrington contended, is their resilient attitude
toward failure. They continue to work hard in a class even
after failing a few tests; when they are stumped or confused by
complex material, they look for new ways to master it rather than
simply giving up. Academic perseverance, in Farrington's formu-
lation, shares certain qualities with noncognitive capacities such
as grit and self-control and delay of gratification. But unlike those
personality traits, which psychologists have shown to be mostly
stable over time, a student's academic perseverance, Farrington
wrote, is highly dependent on context. A student might be
inclined to persevere in school in tenth grade but not eleventh
grade. He might persevere in math class but not history. He might
even persevere on Tuesday but not Wednesday.

The research that Farrington drew on didn't show any
evidence of specific interventions changing a student's innate
level of grit, but there was plenty of evidence that students'
tendency to persevere at academic tasks was highly responsive
to changes in school and classroom contexts. As her report put
it: "The research suggests that, while there may be little return

to trying to make students more gritty as a way of being (i.e., in ways that would carry over to all aspects of their lives at all times and across contexts), students can be influenced to demonstrate perseverant behaviors—such as persisting at academic tasks, seeing big projects through to completion, and buckling down when schoolwork gets hard—in response to certain classroom contexts and under particular psychological conditions."

This was an important distinction: If you were a teacher, you might never be able to get your students to *be* gritty, in the sense of developing some essential character trait called grit. But you could probably make them *act* gritty—to behave in gritty ways. And what Farrington argued was that *that* was exactly what mattered. Those perseverant behaviors would help produce the academic outcomes that you (and your students and society at large) were hoping for.

And what made students act in perseverant ways? Farrington concluded from the research that the key factor behind academic perseverance was students' *academic mindset*—the attitudes and self-perceptions that each child and adolescent possessed. She distilled the voluminous research on student mindset into four key beliefs that contribute most significantly to students' tendency to persevere in the classroom:

1. I belong in this academic community;
2. My ability and competence grow with my effort;
3. I can succeed at this; and
4. This work has value for me.

If students hold these beliefs in mind as they are sitting in math class, Farrington wrote, they are more likely to persevere through the challenges and failures they encounter there. And if they don't, they are more likely to give up at the first sign of trouble.

The complication, of course, is that students who grow up in conditions of adversity are primed, in all sorts of ways, *not* to believe any of Farrington's four statements when they're sitting in math class. This is in part due to the neurobiological effects of adversity, beginning in early childhood. One of the signal results of toxic-stress exposure is a hyperactive fight-or-flight mechanism, which can be a valuable asset in a violent home or neighborhood but is much less helpful during a seventh-grade history lesson. Those fight-or-flight instincts do not encourage in students the soothing belief *I belong here.* Instead, they convey warnings in precisely the opposite direction, at car-alarm volume: "You *don't* belong here. This is enemy territory. Everyone in this school is out to get you." Add to this the fact that children raised in adversity are often, by the time they get to middle or high school, significantly behind their peers academically and dispro- portionately likely to have a history of confrontations with school administrators. In most schools, these are the students placed in remedial classes or subjected to repeated suspensions or both— none of which makes a student likely to feel *I belong here* or *I can succeed at this.*

You can see in Farrington's four academic mindsets echoes of Deci and Ryan's three intrinsic motivations—competence, autonomy, and relatedness. In fact, I think that you can boil

Farrington's list, and Deci and Ryan's, down even further, into just two big meta-messages that are most crucial to student success. The first is concerned with *belonging*—a student's perception that the people in her school, or in her classroom, want her there, that she is a welcome and valued part of that particular learning environment. It is a feeling that depends more than anything on the relationships that she experiences each day at school.

If the first meta-message is about people, the second is about *work*. Students' mindset—their psychology—is also heavily influenced by the work they are asked to do each day in school. Is it challenging? Is it meaningful? Is it within their grasp if they push themselves a little? When a student's schoolwork provides her with a challenge that she can rise to and overcome, she gets a chance to experience, in a way that is hard to reproduce through positive affirmations alone, those much-sought-after Deci-and-Ryanesque feelings of competence and autonomy: *This wasn't easy, but I did it.*

For educators, this framework suggests that there are two toolboxes that are most effective to turn to when you're trying to create an environment conducive to positive student mindsets. The first toolbox has to do with *relationships*: how you treat students, how you talk to them, how you reward and discipline them. The second has to do with *pedagogy*: what you teach, how you teach it, and how you assess whether your students have learned it. In the sections ahead, I'll describe a number of interventions that are improving outcomes among low-income students by enhancing the environments in which they learn. Some target relationships; others focus on pedagogy. As with the early-childhood interventions discussed above, none is perfect. But again, my hope is that, considered together, they might provide us with some broad guidelines, a set of foundational principles, for how best to help students from adverse backgrounds succeed in school.

18. Mindsets

When David Yeager came to Stanford as a psychology graduate student in the mid-2000s, the department was home to some of the biggest names in the psychology of education, including Claude Steele, best known for his discovery of a phenomenon called stereotype threat, and Carol Dweck, famous for her work on student mindset. Stereotype threat refers to the way that individuals who are part of a group vulnerable to stereotypes of underachievement — say, women in an engineering program or black students at an Ivy League university — tend to perform poorly when their anxieties about their identity are triggered. Dweck's fundamental mindset discovery was that students are strongly influenced by implicit and explicit messages about their capacity to grow and improve their intellectual abilities. When they internalize the idea that their intelligence is a static asset, impervious to change, they develop what Dweck calls a fixed mindset, and they tend to shy away from challenges that might expose their perceived intellectual shortcomings. By contrast, when students adopt the "growth mindset" message that intellectual struggle expands one's intellectual ability, they seek out bigger challenges and more advanced work.

Before coming to Stanford, Yeager had taught English at a low-income school in Tulsa, and he was especially motivated to find ways to translate some of this innovative research into practices that could help teachers improve the lives of their students. Today, as a professor at the University of Texas at Austin, Yeager is among the leading researchers exploring how to apply the findings of education psychology in the classroom.

Yeager bases much of his work on the premise that in addition to the neurobiological effects of early adversity, growing up in difficult circumstances often has an effect on children's mental representations of the world as well. Early adversity, Yeager explains, can make children and adolescents more likely to blame themselves for setbacks, more likely to attribute other people's actions to hostility or bias, and more likely to believe that good things, when they do come, will soon be taken away. In collaboration with Stanford professors Geoffrey Cohen and Gregory Walton, Yeager in recent years has been investigating whether and how to intervene with young people whose outlook on the world is dominated by those mental representations.

In a series of experiments, Cohen, Walton, and Yeager have shown the power of what seem to be small-scale mindset interventions — watching a brief video of an older student talking about his struggles with belonging, or reading a magazine article that presents a growth-mindset perspective on brain development—to significantly improve the academic performance of students who are vulnerable to stereotype threat, including low-income students and African-American students.

These experiments have their roots in a technique Cohen developed as an assistant professor at Yale in the late 1990s that he called *wise intervention*—brief, controlled interactions that served to counteract students' fears that their teachers were judging them not as individuals but as members of a stereotyped group. In the classroom, relationships between disadvantaged students and their teachers are often fraught, full of mutual distrust and even antagonism. And the problem can get particularly acute when it comes to a teacher's criticism of a student's work—an indispensable part of good teaching, but an experience that for many disadvantaged students is weighed down by questions of trust: Is my teacher criticizing my work because he's trying to help me improve or because he doesn't respect me? Is he friend or foe? For students from well-off backgrounds, this question, if it comes up at all, is usually answered with a dismissive shrug: Who cares what my teacher thinks about me? For disadvantaged students, however, especially those whose stress-response systems have been compromised by early experiences of adversity, this question can feel vital and urgent, often dominating their experience of school.

In a landmark experiment in 2006, Cohen and a colleague, Julio Garcia, tested a wise intervention designed to counteract this anxiety with a group of underachieving seventh-graders at a suburban middle school in New England. The students were assigned to write an essay describing a personal hero. Each essay was corrected by the students' regular classroom teacher, marked up in the usual way with questions and suggestions for revision written in the margin.

Cohen and Garcia then randomly divided the students into a control group and a treatment group. On each student's marked-up paper, they attached a note the size of a Post-it with a sentence in the teacher's handwriting. The control group's Post-it read, "I'm giving you these comments so that you'll have feedback on your paper" — a bland and self-evident statement. The treatment group's Post-it, though, was more interesting; it drew on Cohen's finding that the most effective (or "wise") way to intervene with students who might be anxious about their ability or their sense of belonging is to combine, within a single message, high expectations and assurance that with effort the student can meet those high expectations. The treatment Post-it was an explicit expression of those twin messages. It read simply, "I'm giving you these comments because I have very high expectations and I know that you can reach them."

Students got their papers back with the teacher's comments and the Post-it, and then they were given the option of revising their essay to respond to the comments and improve their grade. White students in the class, who had little reason to think that they might be judged according to the teacher's stereotyped view of their race, were slightly more likely to revise their paper if they received the "high expectations" Post-it, but the effect on them was quite small. Among the black students, however, the treatment and control groups behaved wildly differently.

Just 17 percent of the black students who received the bland "so you'll have feedback" Post-it revised their paper, compared with 72 percent of those who got the "high expectations" Post-it. In a second, parallel study in which all students were required to revise their paper, the black students who received the "high expectations" Post-it were graded more than two points higher, on a 15-point scale, on the revised essay than the ones who got the plain-vanilla "feedback" Post-it. In other words, the message on the "high expectations" Post-it — a single sentence, remember — not only made the students far more likely to revise their work, but it made them more likely to improve their essays substantially when they did.

What was behind this remarkable result? Yeager, who later collaborated with Cohen on a replication of the New England results, theorizes that the message on the Post-it had the effect of switching off, at a critical time, the clanging fight-or-flight alarm sounding in the students' heads. At the very moment when a student might be gearing up to react to the teacher's comments as a threat, a sign of the teacher's personal disapproval or bias, the Post-it gave the student an alternative frame through which to view those comments — not as an attack, in other words, but as a vote of confidence that the student was capable of high-quality work.

* * *

19. Relationships

For Yeager, the conclusion to draw from the study is not that teachers should start slapping high-expectations Post-its on every piece of work they hand back to students. It's that teachers have a critical and potentially transformative opportunity, when dealing with students who perceive school as a threatening place, to disarm those threats by changing the way they communicate. For some students, it may take only a relatively minor shift in tone to build that trust. That's what the Post-it study seems to suggest, at least. But for other students, those whose backgrounds have led them to experience that fight-or-flight reaction not just in occasional high-stress moments but all the time, developing a sense of belonging and connection in school may require a more immersive intervention.

Jens Ludwig, an economist at the University of Chicago who oversees a research group there called the Crime Lab, has for the past few years been studying, along with some colleagues, a counseling program called Becoming a Man, or BAM, which operates inside 49 Chicago schools, mostly high schools in low-income neighborhoods. BAM uses group discussions and role-playing exercises to help develop anger-management and self-control capacities in the students, all teenage boys, who are selected for the program because they are considered to be at especially high risk of dropout or of involvement with the criminal-justice system or both. Ludwig has evaluated BAM in a series of randomized controlled trials, and he has shown that the program reduced participants' involvement in violent crime by 44 percent and at the same time improved students' grades, attendance, and predicted graduation rate. BAM seems to work by influencing the important mental functions that a stress-filled childhood tends to impair, like impulse control and the ability to successfully manage aggressive feelings.

Last spring, in a classroom at Roberto Clemente Community Academy, a high school in Chicago's West Town neighborhood, I sat in on a Becoming a Man discussion between eight juniors and Brandon Bailys, the group leader. The students were all black or Latino, but beyond that commonality they were surprisingly diverse: One student had gang tattoos on his neck; another sat slouched in his chair, a mess of dreadlocks covering his face; two others with modified Goth haircuts were excited about attending a comic-book convention at McCormick Place the following weekend. Bailys, who is 28, was trained as a therapist, but he looks more like a wrestler, short and stocky and energetic, and he led the group, which had been meeting once a week for two years, with a light but steady hand.

The session began with each member of the group doing a "check-in," describing how he was feeling that day physically, intellectually, spiritually, and emotionally. Then, for 50 minutes, the young men talked, with Bailys loosely guiding the conversation around the theme of what it takes to go "outside of the box" in your thinking and decision-making—a topic that was broad

enough to encompass both a discussion about what it might
feel like to leave Illinois for college and a long debate about the
experience that Rashid, one of the group members, had had the
previous weekend, when he was jumped by two guys while he was
walking from his grandmother's house to a convenience store to
buy M&M's. The young men didn't always see eye to eye, but the
connection and trust they felt, with each other and with Bailys,
was plain to see.

When I spoke with Bailys after the meeting, he told me that
many of the young men in the group I observed, and in the four
other BAM groups that he guides at Clemente, are coping with
significant experiences of trauma, both past and present. He was
on his way, after we talked, to the principal's office to counsel
a young man in one of his groups who had been burning and
cutting himself to numb his emotional pain. Though the meeting
I attended seemed on the surface like an informal discussion, to
Bailys it was akin to group therapy. He told me he sometimes
employed strategies from gestalt therapy, like the empty-chair
technique (in which a young man addresses an empty chair
representing his absent father), to help the boys deal with the
"father wounds" that, Bailys said, exerted such a powerful influence on their lives.

Turnaround for Children, the school-transformation
nonprofit that produced the building-blocks paper I wrote about
earlier, tries to address similar wounds in the young people it
serves. But rather than diagnose those wounds using the language
of gestalt therapy, Turnaround — which is currently contracted to
work in seven schools in New York City, two in Newark, and two

in Washington, D.C. — draws primarily on our scientific knowledge of the biological effects of a disadvantaged childhood.

According to Turnaround's research, many of the behavior-
management challenges that educators in high-poverty schools
face are due to the combustible combination, in the classroom, of
two cohorts of students. The first is a small group of students who
have experienced high levels of toxic stress (and likely have high
ACE scores) and as a result are angry and rebellious and disruptive. This group, Turnaround estimates, represents between 10
and 15 percent of the student body in most high-poverty schools.
Students in the second cohort have also experienced adversity
and stress, but not to the same degree. They are less likely to start
trouble, but their highly sensitive fight-or-flight mechanisms are
easily triggered when trouble comes.

Turnaround was founded and is run by Pamela Cantor, a
child psychiatrist. And when Turnaround is contracted to work
at a particular school, its intervention team, usually three or
four people, starts by addressing the psychological needs of that
inner core of potentially disruptive students, sometimes offering
them on-site counseling and mentoring, often referring them and
their families to mental-health services like individual or family
therapy elsewhere in the community (while they remain students
at the school). Turnaround's staff then turns its attention to the
classroom environment as a whole, coaching teachers on strategies to improve students' academic outcomes by improving their
experience in class. There are echoes, in this element of Turnaround's work, of the coaching that the prekindergarten teachers
in the Chicago School Readiness Project received, and even of the

coaching that parents get in ABC and FIND. Teachers are trained in behavior-management techniques that dial confrontations down rather than up, and they are given strategies to help them create a climate of belonging and engagement in the classroom.

Turnaround's leaders don't yet have the data to show what kind of effect this approach has had on the schools with which they're partnering. But a recent study by Joseph Allen, a psychology professor at the University of Virginia, and Robert C. Pianta, the dean of the education school there, demonstrates that when teachers are trained in how to create a better environment in the classroom, that can have a measurable effect on student performance. Allen and Pianta conducted a randomized controlled trial with 78 secondary school teachers at schools across Virginia. The teachers in the treatment group were coached for a full school year using a system called My Teaching Partner. The focus of the training, delivered via professional-development workshops and phone-coaching sessions, was the personal interactions in the classroom between teachers and students; the coaches gave teachers strategies designed to help them build a "positive emotional climate" and show "sensitivity to student needs for autonomy."

The following year, students in classes taught by teachers in the treatment group scored significantly better than students in other classes on the relevant Virginia state assessment, rising on average from the 50th percentile to the 59th percentile in the state as a whole. The results were like an echo of what happened with the four-year-olds enrolled in the Chicago School Readiness Project. As in the CSRP experiment, the teachers in Virginia didn't receive any training in how to deliver academic contact, only in how to interact with students in a positive way. Again, though, as their approach to their students changed, the classroom climate improved, and their students' test scores went up.

20. Pedagogy

What is most interesting to me about Turnaround for Children is that, unlike BAM, Turnaround's intervention involves not only the relationship toolbox but also the pedagogical toolbox: the actual teaching and learning that goes on in the classroom. In the spring of 2015, I visited M.S. 45 in the Bronx, a high-poverty public school where Turnaround had been working for about a year. For the first few months of its contract, while the Turnaround social worker assigned to the school spent her time identifying the highest-need students and connecting them with mental-health and counseling services, Turnaround's instructional coaches concentrated on classroom management, helping teachers create and communicate clear expectations and rules, and consistent consequences for violating those rules, and providing them with tools to help de-escalate conflicts when they did arise. But then, once a basic level of calm prevailed in the school, the coaches turned their attention to encouraging

what they called cooperative learning, a pedagogical approach
that promoted student engagement in the learning process:
less lecture time; fewer repetitive worksheets; more time spent
working in small groups, solving problems, engaging in discussions, and collaborating on longer-term creative projects.

For many teachers at M.S. 45, the Turnaround coaches told
me, embracing this part of the Turnaround model was much
more challenging than adopting the new classroom-management
strategies. Giving students more autonomy in their learning
meant giving up control—handing over the reins of the classroom. And like many other teachers at high-poverty schools,
those at M.S. 45 had come to believe that with students as
potentially disruptive as theirs, strong, dominant teacher control
was the only way to keep the classroom calm and orderly;
handing over the reins would mean chaos. But Turnaround's
coaches eventually persuaded the teachers, after months of
professional-development sessions, classroom observations, and
one-on-one conversations, that giving students more opportunity
to experience autonomy, and to engage more deeply in their
own learning, would actually make the climate in the classrooms
calmer, not crazier.

That principle was embraced quite readily by the teachers
at another school I visited in the spring of 2015: Polaris Charter
Academy on Chicago's West Side. Polaris is affiliated with a
national nonprofit called EL Education. (The organization was
known as Expeditionary Learning until last October, when
it changed its name.) There are more than 150 schools in the
EL Education network, and they represent a diverse variety

of settings: urban and rural, charter and traditional public, high-poverty and middle-class. Within the EL network, Polaris, which enrolls students from kindergarten through eighth grade, has one of the more disadvantaged student bodies: 91 percent of the students are eligible for a free or reduced-price lunch, and the neighborhood where the school is located, West Humboldt Park, has high rates of violent crime, unemployment, and poverty.

In recent years, I have visited EL schools in Chicago, Washington, and New York City. What keeps drawing me back to the EL model is that, like Turnaround, it explicitly utilizes both of the toolboxes I described above: relationships and pedagogy. On the relationship side, the most important institution at EL schools is called Crew, an ongoing, multiyear discussion and advisory group for students. The Expeditionary Learning model was developed 25 years ago out of a collaboration between the Harvard Graduate School of Education and Outward Bound USA, and the Outward Bound principle of building confidence and knowledge through shared challenges is still at the heart of the EL model. Kurt Hahn, the founder of Outward Bound, is famous for his slogan "We are crew, not passengers," and it is from this maxim that EL's tradition takes its name. Each EL student is assigned to a crew, which meets every day for half an hour or so to discuss matters important to the students, both academic and personal. In middle school and high school, the groups are relatively intimate—10 or 15 kids—and students generally stay in the same crew for two years or longer, with the same teacher leading the group year after year. As a result, many EL students will tell you that their crew is the place at school where they most feel a sense of belonging;

for some of them, it's the place where they most feel a sense of belonging, period.

On the morning I visited Polaris, I sat in on a sixth-grade crew meeting led by a teacher named Molly Brady, who had been at the school for six years. It was a Monday, the first day back after a three-week school break, and Brady first had the students go around in a circle, greeting and shaking the hand of the person next to them and asking how their break had been; students responded with "green," "yellow," or "red," for good, OK, or terrible. Though these students here were five years younger than the ones I'd observed at Clemente, the meeting was in many ways reminiscent of that BAM conversation—respectful, familiar, loose, cycling back and forth between the immediate concerns of the day and big-picture questions like "How do we live out our ideals?" and "What do we want for ourselves when we leave Polaris?"

This particular crew had been together, guided by Brady, for three straight years, and when I spoke to Brady afterward she explained that those years had given her a fairly intimate understanding of the group and its dynamics, which allowed her to tailor each day's activities to the particular needs of the students. One boy, a new arrival at Polaris that year, had been kicked out of his previous school for breaking into the principal's office, and while he was doing better at Polaris, Brady said, he had clearly not left his troubles behind; he was the only student during the round of handshakes and greetings to report (in a quiet voice) that his spring break had been red. Brady didn't draw attention to his answer, but she paired him with another boy who she felt might be a good match for his mood, and she made a point of talking with him after the crew meeting to make sure he was OK.

Crew is the centerpiece of EL's strategy for surrounding students with an environment of supportive relationships. But the more significant element of the EL formula to me is on the pedagogical side of the equation, in its distinctive academic practices. Classrooms at Polaris and other EL schools are by design much more engaging and interactive than classrooms in most other American public schools. They are full of student discussions and group activities large and small; teachers guide the conversation, but they spend much less time lecturing than most public school teachers do. EL students complete a lot of rigorous and demanding long-term projects, often going through extensive and repeated revisions based on critiques from teachers and peers. They frequently work on these projects in collaborative groups, and often a project will conclude with students giving a presentation in front of the class, the school, or even a community group. In addition, students are responsible, whenever possible, for assessing themselves; twice a year, at report-card time, parents or other family members come in to the school for meetings known as student-led conferences, in which students as young as five narrate for their parents and teacher their achievements and struggles over the past semester.

The pedagogical guru behind EL's instructional practices and curriculum is Ron Berger, the organization's chief academic officer. Berger, who spent 25 years working as a public school teacher and educational consultant in rural Massachusetts before joining Expeditionary Learning, clearly feels a special connection with those EL schools, like Polaris, that enroll high numbers of students growing up in adversity. When we spoke, he explained that this feeling of connection is rooted in his own childhood, growing up along with four siblings in a chaotic and unstable family. That adversity took a toll, he told me; some of his siblings have faced and continue to face crises and challenges in adulthood. As a result, he said, he knows firsthand how the stress and trauma of an unstable home can unsettle and derail a child's development, and he understands that without the right intervention, children may never recover from those early setbacks.

Expeditionary Learning schools have been shown, in independent studies, to have a significant positive effect on academic progress. A 2013 study by Mathematica Policy Research revealed that students at five urban EL middle schools advanced ahead of matched peers at comparison schools by an average of ten months in math and seven months in reading over the course of three years. The research also shows that an EL education has a greater positive impact on low-income students than on other students.

Berger is not surprised by that latter fact; he has a clear sense of how and why the model works for children growing up in adversity. "When kids have been damaged emotionally, they can instantiate that into their own personal identity in different ways," he told me. "Some kids get withdrawn and protective. Other kids get this kind of shell of being a tough guy, and they're frozen in school. Either way it restricts them from being able to contribute in class, to be a part of discussions, to raise their hand, to show that they care about their learning. It holds back any kind of passion or interaction. They can't take risks in school, and you can't learn if you're not taking risks." Berger recognizes these behaviors, he said, because they are exactly what he himself did when he was a kid. He didn't let anyone at school know what was happening at home; he kept his two lives entirely separate. He showed up at school, he did the work, but he wasn't really there.

Students at EL schools, Berger said, can't hide in the way that he did. Crew helps pull them out of their shells, and in class they're compelled on a daily basis to interact with their peers and teachers in group discussions and to collaborate on group projects, and before long that kind of interaction begins to feel natural. When I visited another EL school last spring, the Washington Heights Expeditionary Learning School (known as WHEELS) in Upper Manhattan, almost every classroom I visited was engaged in some kind of elaborate discussion or creative project that demanded involvement from every student. In one seventh-grade social-science class, the students were clustered in groups of four, working together with magic markers on a big poster. They had been assigned to represent either the Federalist or the Republican party during the constitutional debates of the 1790s, and they covered their posters with slogans and arguments supporting the case for their vision of government, preparing for a class-wide debate. The teacher glided from table to table, asking questions and offering advice, but for the most part the students organized themselves. I couldn't help but be struck by the unusual fact that these were middle school students studying U.S. history, and that they seemed to be having genuine fun.

What's more, these students were among the most disadvantaged in the New York City public school system. One hundred percent of the student population at WHEELS has a family income that falls below the federal cutoff for lunch subsidies, and 99 percent of them are Latino or African-American. They are a demographic, in other words, that in many big-city middle and high schools is seen as a behavioral challenge and an academic liability. In social-science class that day, however, they were learning complex material and behaving perfectly well — and not because they were incentivized with rewards or threatened with punishments, but because school was, for that period at least, actually kind of interesting.

Teachers and administrators at EL schools talk quite a bit about character — their term for noncognitive skills. The central premise of EL schools is that character is built not through lectures or direct instruction from teachers but through the experience of persevering through challenging academic work. "You can't teach character by just telling kids to be more confident or self-assured or have more intellectual courage," Berger told me. "The way kids learn that is by continually being compelled and supported to take risks — by sharing their work with their parents, by sharing their work with groups, by speaking out in class, by presenting their work. When they first have to engage like that, they are nervous, they need support, they cry — but eventually they develop the confidence and they do it. And those opportunities are what build their character."

This, to me, is the most significant innovation in the work that is going on at EL schools. In general, when schools try to address the impact that a stress-filled childhood might have on disadvantaged students, the first — and often the only — toolbox they turn to is the relationship one. And while it's certainly true that those students need the sense of belonging and connection that comes from feeling embedded in school within a web of deep and close relationships, the critical insight of Expeditionary Learning is that belonging alone isn't enough. In order for a student to truly feel motivated by and about school, he also has to perceive that he is doing important work—work that is challenging, rigorous, and deep.

Meeting and overcoming meaningful academic challenges is critical to developing the other positive academic mindsets that Camille Farrington described, like *I can succeed at this* and *My ability and competence grow with my effort.* This is, in fact, what Farrington found most effectively produces positive mindsets in kids, especially disadvantaged kids: the experience of encountering a problem you don't know how to solve, struggling with it (often with the help of a team of peers, support from a teacher, or both) and then finally figuring it out. When students get a chance to experience those moments, no one has to persuade them, in an abstract or theoretical way, of the principles of a growth mindset. They intuitively believe that their brains grow through effort and struggle, and they believe it for the best possible reason: because they can feel it happening.

* * *

21. Challenge

The experience of persisting through an intellectual challenge and succeeding despite the struggle is a profound one for school-children — as profound, it seems, as serve-and-return is for the infant brain. It produces feelings of both competence and auto-nomy — two of Deci and Ryan's three big intrinsic motivations. And yet most of our schools, especially schools educating poor kids, operate in ways that steer children away from those experiences.

In 2007, Robert Pianta of the University of Virginia published in *Science* the results of a large-scale survey of American public schools that he and a team of researchers had undertaken, observing regular instruction over the course of an entire school day in 737 typical fifth-grade classrooms across the United States, as well as hundreds of additional first- and third-grade classrooms. Pianta's researchers found that in almost every school they observed, the instruction students received was repetitive and undemanding, limited mostly to the endless practice of basic skills. Cooperative learning and small-group instruction — the central pedagogical strategies of groups like Turnaround and schools like Polaris and WHEELS — were rare, taking up less than 5 percent of classroom time, and so were opportunities for students to practice or develop analytic skills like critical thinking, deep reading, or complex problem-solving. Instead, students spent most of their time hearing lectures on basic skills from teachers or practicing those basic skills on worksheets. The average fifth-grade student received five times as much instruction in basic skills as instruction focused on problem-solving or reasoning, Pianta and his coauthors reported; in first and third grades, the ratio was ten to one.

And while the *Science* authors found instruction to be basic and repetitive even in American schools with a mostly middle-class or upper-middle-class student population, they found that the situation was considerably worse in schools that enrolled a lot of low-income children. Students in schools populated mostly by middle-class-and-above children were about equally likely to find themselves in a classroom with engaged and interesting instruction (47 percent of students) as in one with basic, repetitive instruction (53 percent of students). But students in schools serving mostly low-income children were almost all (91 percent) in classrooms marked by basic, uninteresting teaching.

It's important to note that this approach to education, so widespread in the United States, is not inevitable. In other countries, classroom teaching can look quite different. In the 1990s, a researcher named James Stigler coordinated a vast international project that involved videotaping the classrooms of hundreds of randomly selected eighth-grade math teachers in the United States, Germany, and Japan. Stigler, who summarized his research in a 1999 book that he coauthored with James Hiebert titled *The Teaching Gap,* found that math classes in Japan almost always followed a very different script from math classes in the United States.

In Japan, teachers would introduce a new mathematical
method—let's say, adding fractions with different denominators,
like ⅗ + ½ —by presenting the students with a problem they'd
never seen before and instructing them to figure it out on their
own. Students would stare at the problem for a while, scratch
their heads, sometimes wince in pain, and then come up with an
answer that was usually wrong.

Next would come a series of discussions, in small groups
and in the class as a whole, in which students compared and
contrasted their solutions, arguing and lobbying for different
approaches. The teacher would guide the discussion in a way that
led, eventually, to a new element of math understanding (in this
case, the principle of finding the lowest common denominator).
Often the correct solution would be proposed not by the teacher
but by one of the students. The whole process was sometimes
bewildering and occasionally frustrating for students, but
that was kind of the point. By the end of class, confusion and
frustration gave way to the satisfaction of a new depth of comprehension, not delivered in whole cloth by an omniscient adult,
but constructed from the ground up, in part through a dialogue
among students.

In American classrooms, by contrast, Stigler found that a
unit on adding fractions with unlike denominators would usually
begin with the teacher writing on an overhead projector a reliable
formula to solve the problem, which students would be expected
to copy down, memorize, and use for each subsequent problem.
The teacher would then complete, on the overhead projector, a
couple of sample problems while the students watched, listened,

and copied the problems down in their workbooks. The teacher would then give the students a series of exercises to complete on their own that looked very similar to the sample problems the teacher had just demonstrated. Students would absorb these new procedures, Stigler and Hiebert wrote in *The Teaching Gap*, by "practicing them many times, with later exercises being slightly more difficult than earlier ones." The guiding principle for American teachers seemed to be that "practice should be relatively error-free, with high levels of success at each point. Confusion and frustration, in this traditional American view, should be minimized."

Stigler's researchers logged hundreds of hours of videotape, which allowed them to assign some hard numbers to these cultural tendencies. In Japan, 41 percent of students' time in math class was still spent on basic practice—churning through one problem after another—but 44 percent was devoted to more creative stuff: inventing new procedures or adapting familiar procedures to unfamiliar material. In the American classrooms, by contrast, 96 percent of students' time was spent on repetitive practice, and less than 1 percent was spent puzzling through new approaches.

This dominant American instructional strategy may save students from those uncomfortable feelings of confusion and struggle that Japanese students must endure—but it also denies them the character-building opportunities that Ron Berger described. In the same way that the zero-tolerance approach to discipline sends precisely the opposite psychological message to disadvantaged kids than what we now know they need in order to feel motivated and engaged with school, so do many basic elements of traditional American pedagogy work in direct opposition to what the psychological research tells us will help those children succeed.

22. Deeper Learning

The pedagogical techniques that prevail at EL schools and that Turnaround's instructional coaches emphasize in their work are connected to a larger trend in education today, known colloquially as deeper learning. This relatively new movement, which is also sometimes called student-centered learning, has its roots in the progressive strain of American educational thought, but its current incarnation is also based on the modern belief, common among corporate executives and other business leaders, that there is a major and potentially calamitous disconnect brewing between the historical structures and traditions of the American public school system and the labor-force demands of the 21st-century American economy. When most of our current pedagogical practices were developed more than a century ago, the essential economic purpose of public schools was to produce industrial workers who were fast and reliable when assigned repetitive mechanical or clerical tasks. In this century, deeper-learning proponents argue, the job market requires a very different set of skills, one that our current educational system is not configured to help students develop: the ability to work in teams, to present ideas to a group, to write effectively, to think deeply and analytically about problems, to take information and techniques learned in one context and adapt them to a new and unfamiliar problem or situation. In order to develop those skills, advocates say, students need opportunities to practice them in school. And right now, in most schools, they don't get those opportunities.

And so deeper-learning proponents promote inquiry-based instruction, which means that in the classroom, teachers tend to engage students in discussions rather than just lecturing to them; project-based learning, in which students spend much of their time working, often in groups, on elaborate projects that might take weeks or months to complete; and performance-based assessments, in which students are judged not primarily by their scores on end-of-semester exams, but by the portfolios, presentations, artwork, and written work they produce throughout the year. At many schools run on deeper-learning principles, there is an ethos that celebrates peer critique, revision, and tinkering; student work often goes through many drafts over the course of the school year, based on feedback from teachers and classmates. One of the fundamental beliefs of deeper-learning advocates is that these practices — revising work over and over, with frequent critiques; persisting at long-term projects; dealing with the frustrations of hands-on experimentation — develop not just students' content knowledge and intellectual ability, but their noncognitive capacities as well: what Camille Farrington would call academic perseverance and what others might call grit or resilience.

There are plenty of deeper-learning skeptics out there, and one of their chief concerns is that while project-based learning in the hands of a well-trained educator can be used in the classroom in a highly effective way, it is also a technique that is easy for an unprepared teacher to do quite badly. In order to be worthwhile, student projects need to be rigorously planned, carefully supported, and built on a foundation of accurate and relevant information. When that doesn't happen, project-based learning can become the empty calories of education: a collection of engaging distractions that are unrelated to the larger goal of increasing students' knowledge.

Still, perhaps the most significant shortcoming of the deeper-learning movement today is that you are much more likely to find these ideas in use if you visit a school in a well-off neighborhood than if you visit a school in a poor one. In 2014, Jal Mehta, a professor at the Harvard Graduate School of Education, wrote a provocative essay, published online by *Education Week,* titled "Deeper Learning Has a Race Problem." In it he identified some worrisome issues not only of race but of class. "Deeper learning has historically been the province of the advantaged — those who could afford to send their children to the best private schools and to live in the most desirable school districts," Mehta wrote. "Research on both inequality across schools and tracking within schools has suggested that students in more affluent schools and top tracks are given the kind of problem-solving education that befits the future managerial class, whereas students in lower tracks and higher-poverty schools are given the kind of rule-following tasks that mirror much of factory and other working-class work."

Mehta acknowledged in his essay that some of this inequity is on the supply side: Schools that have the freedom and resources to adopt the techniques of deeper learning are more likely to be well-funded independent schools or public schools in wealthy suburbs or neighborhoods. But a significant part of the divide, he wrote, is on the demand side. Many of those who are most committed to the education of low-income and minority students — including many of the parents of those students — are skeptical that deeper-learning methods are the best ones for disadvantaged students. Those skeptics (and others) point out that in the 1960s and 1970s, "project-based learning" was used in some low-income schools as a euphemism for the practice of having poor kids build Lego models and doodle in coloring books while the rich kids across town learned how to read and do math. They also express concern that students without the deep and broad background knowledge and fluency that affluent children generally absorb from their homes and communities first need to develop that core knowledge before they can benefit from a collaborative, project-based approach.

Bob Lenz is the co-founder of the Envision Schools network of charters, which has made project-based learning the central pedagogical strategy in its four schools in the San Francisco Bay Area, all of which serve mostly low-income black and Latino students. In his 2015 book *Transforming Schools*, Lenz addressed the class concerns that many people have about the

deeper-learning approach. "We do encounter skeptics when
we describe what we do," he wrote. "Project-based learning is a
luxury, people will say, for the well-resourced and well-prepared
upper-middle class, but kids on the wrong side of the achievement gap can't afford to waste time on projects when there is so
much work to do in shoring up their basic skills." Lenz disagrees.
"We have yet to encounter a single student who was either not
ready or somehow too advanced for the kind of performance- and
project-based education that we advocate," he wrote.

There is a growing body of empirical evidence that suggests
that Lenz is right: deeper-learning methods, when employed well,
do actually produce measurable benefits for students in poverty.
As I mentioned above, Expeditionary Learning schools have
shown significant academic success with low-income students.
Graduates of Envision Schools are persisting in college at high
rates (though the schools are new enough that that data is still
preliminary). And a 2014 study of student performance at schools
in California and New York, conducted by the American Insti-
tutes for Research, found that attending deeper-learning schools
had a significant positive impact, on average, on students' content
knowledge and standardized-test scores. (Three-fifths of the
students in the study were low-income, and their scores improved
just as much as the scores of the students who were above the
low-income cutoff.)

Deeper-learning strategies are often presented as a corrective
to the no-excuses philosophy of education associated with some
of the earliest and best-known charter-school networks, including
KIPP, Uncommon Schools, and Achievement First. In their early

years, especially, those schools, which serve mostly low-income students and often achieve standardized-test scores that are far above average for such students, emphasized strict behavior codes, requiring students to comply with a rigorous set of rules about how to dress and how to sit in the classroom and how to walk through the hallways. At many of those schools, elaborate systems of incentives and punishments were (and often still are) a central part of the strategy for managing and motivating students.

But more recently, the sharp dividing lines that once existed between no-excuses and deeper-learning schools have begun to blur. In the fall of 2015, Elm City Preparatory Elementary School in New Haven, Connecticut, one of the founding schools of the Achievement First network, introduced a wholesale redesign of its curriculum that includes an embrace of many of the beliefs and practices of deeper learning, including an increased emphasis on experiential learning and student autonomy. Students at Elm City (86 percent of whom qualify for free or reduced-price lunch) now control their schedule and follow their own personal interests in their learning much more than they used to, and they have more autonomy in the subjects they study, including daily "enrichment" courses in robotics, dance, and tae kwon do. Once every two months, Elm City teachers lead students on a two-week "expeditionary" project in which they deeply study a single subject, sometimes involving extensive time outside school visiting a farm, museum, or historical site.

When I spoke in December 2015 to Dacia Toll, the co-CEO and co-founder of Achievement First, she said the Elm City experiment, which had been under way for only a few months, had taken some getting used to by teachers and administrators. She and her redesign team had been heavily influenced by the motivation research of Deci and Ryan, which, you'll recall, emphasized three crucial intrinsic motivators: autonomy, competence, and relatedness. "The hardest one for us at Achievement First has always been autonomy," Toll said. "In the past, we've had a tendency to think we know what's best for students. So letting kids choose what to focus on has been a bit of a challenge for us." So far, though, she said, the experiment had been a success. Students were still getting the rigorous education that Elm City had become known for, but now they were more motivated, more enthusiastic, and more engaged.

23. Solutions

When you visit a school like WHEELS or Polaris, it is hard not to feel hopeful, not just for the prospects of the students there, but for the possibility that a new approach to educating low-income children, rooted in the science of adversity, might be taking hold more broadly. I felt the same sense of hope observing ABC's parent coaches and All Our Kin's childcare mentors at work, patiently spreading a new set of ideas about the environments that infants and toddlers need to thrive.

But the reality is that the ideas I've explored in this book are still outside the mainstream, and the interventions I've described are still quite rare. Most preschools and schools that serve low-income children in this country don't operate anything like Educare or Polaris. The early-childhood organizations whose work I highlighted in the first half of this book are all still small in scale, serving at most a few thousand children or families. The schools and classroom interventions that I've described educate a tiny fraction of the nation's poor children, and they are competing against a dominant culture in education that only very rarely considers whether there might be another, better way to motivate and engage children who are growing up in poverty.

The system that exists today in the United States to support and educate those children is profoundly broken. There are currently more than 15 million American children living below the poverty line, and almost 7 million of them are living in deep poverty, with family incomes of less than $12,000 a year for a family of four. The problems most of these children face are relentless and pervasive. Statistically, they are likely to live in chaotic, disrupted families, in neighborhoods or regions of concentrated poverty where there are few resources to nurture children and countless perils to wound them, physically or psychologically or both. The schools they attend are likely to be segregated by race and class and to have less money to spend on instruction than the schools well-off students attend, and their teachers are likely to be less experienced and less well-trained than teachers at other schools.

Faced with the depth of this disadvantage, the intervention

strategies I've described in this report can seem overmatched. But what the research I've described here makes clear is that intervening in the lives of disadvantaged children — by educating them better in school, helping their parents support them better at home, or, ideally, some combination of the two — is the most effective and promising anti-poverty strategy we have. When poor children grow up in an environment marked by stable, responsive parenting; by schools that make them feel a sense of belonging and purpose; and by classroom teachers who challenge and support them, they thrive, and their opportunities for a successful life increase exponentially.

Which brings us back to the question that I raised at the beginning of this book: *Now that we know this, what do we do?*

Let me propose three answers.

First, we need to change our policies. Consistently creating what Pamela Cantor has called "fortified environments" for poor children will mean fundamentally rethinking and remaking many of our entrenched institutions and practices: how we provide aid to low-income parents; how we create, fund, and manage systems of early-childhood care and education; how we train our teachers; how we discipline our students and assess their learning; and how we run our schools. These are essentially questions of public policy, and if real solutions are going to be found to the problems of disadvantaged children, these questions will need to be addressed, in a creative and committed way, by public officials at all levels — by school superintendents, school-board members, mayors, governors, and cabinet secretaries — as well as by individual citizens, community groups, and philanthropists across the

When we hear the word *environment*, we often think first of a child's physical environment. And adverse physical surroundings do play a role in children's development, especially when they are literally toxic, as when children are exposed to lead in their drinking water or carbon monoxide in the air they breathe. But one of the most important findings of this new cohort of researchers is that for most children, the environmental factors that matter most have less to do with the buildings they live in than with the relationships they experience – the way the adults in their lives interact with them, especially in times of stress.

The first and most essential environment where children develop their emotional and psychological and cognitive capacities is the home — and, more specifically, the family. Beginning in infancy, children rely on responses from their parents to make sense of the world. Researchers at the Center on the Developing Child at Harvard University have labeled these "serve and return" interactions. Infants make a sound or look at an object — that's the serve — and parents return the serve by sharing the child's attention and responding to his babbles and cries with gestures, facial expressions, and speech: "Yes, that's your doggy!" "Do you see the fan?" "Oh dear, are you sad?" These rudimentary interactions between parents and babies, which can often feel to parents nonsensical and repetitive, are for the infants full of valuable information about what the world is going to be like. More than any other experiences infants have, they trigger the development and strengthening of neural connections in the brain between the regions that control emotion, cognition, language, and memory.

A second crucial role parents play early on is as external

regulators of their children's stress, in both good ways and bad. Research has shown that when parents behave harshly or unpredictably — especially at moments when their children are upset — the children are less likely over time to develop the ability to manage strong emotions and more likely to respond ineffectively to stressful situations. By contrast, parents who are able to help their children handle stressful moments and calm themselves down after a tantrum or a scare often have a profoundly positive effect on the children's long-term ability to manage stress. Infancy and early childhood are naturally full of crying jags and meltdowns, and each one is, for the child, a learning opportunity (even if that's hard to believe, in the moment, for the child's parents). When a child's caregivers respond to her jangled emotions in a sensitive and measured way, she is more likely to learn that she herself has the capacity to manage and cope with her feelings, even intense and unpleasant ones. That understanding, which is not primarily an intellectual understanding but instead is etched deep into the child's psyche, will prove immensely valuable when the next stressful situation comes along — or even in the face of a crisis years in the future.

Neuroscientists have over the past decade uncovered evidence, both in rodent and human studies, that parental caregiving, especially in moments of stress, affects children's development not only on the level of hormones and brain chemicals, but even more deeply, on the level of gene expression. Researchers at McGill University have shown that specific parenting behaviors by mother rats change the way certain chemicals are affixed to certain sequences on a baby rat's DNA, a country. I've tried in these pages to identify some specific changes in funding and policy that I think will enable us to help more children more effectively. But beyond those concrete suggestions, my larger aspiration for this book is that it might provide us with a set of guiding principles to propel forward the public-policy discussions and debates that we need to have now.

Second, we need to change our practices. The project of creating better environments for children growing up in adversity is, at bottom, the work of individuals. Which means that the teachers, mentors, social workers, coaches, and parents who spend their days working with low-income children don't need to wait for large-scale policy changes to be enacted in order to take actions today and tomorrow and the next day that will help those children succeed. What the research I've described here makes clear, I hope, is that the trajectory that children's lives follow can sometimes be redirected by things that might at first seem, to the adults in their lives, to be small and insignificant. The tone of a parent's voice. The words a teacher writes on a Post-it note. The way a math class is organized. The extra time that a mentor or a coach takes to listen to a child facing a challenge. Those personal actions can create powerful changes, and those individual changes can resonate on a national scale.

Finally, we need to change our way of thinking. When you spend time reading through the kind of intervention studies that I've written about here, it's easy to get caught up in the specifics of the data: sample sizes, standard deviations, regression analyses. And that data certainly matters. But I also find it useful, every once in a while, to think about the individual people who conducted these studies: the doctors or psychologists or social workers who went in to an orphanage in Russia or an impoverished neighborhood in Jamaica or a high school in Chicago or a living room in Queens and said, in essence, *I want to help. I think we can do better.*

As much as we draw on the data that those researchers have produced, I think we can also draw on their example. The premise underlying their work is that if there are children suffering in your community — or your nation — there is something you can do to help. We all still have a lot to learn about how best to deliver that help, which means that we need to continue and indeed expand upon the work those researchers are doing. But at the same time, we don't need to know exactly what to do in order to know that we need to do something.

Helping children in adversity to transcend their difficult circumstances is hard and often painful work. It can be depressing, discouraging — even infuriating. But what the research shows is that it can also make a tremendous difference, not only in the lives of individual children and their families, but in our communities and our nation as a whole. It is work we can all do, whether or not it is the profession we have chosen. The first step is simply to embrace the idea, as those researchers did, that we can do better.

ACKNOWLEDGMENTS

This book was written with the generous support of five philanthropic organizations: the CityBridge Foundation, the Joyce Foundation, the Raikes Foundation, the Bainum Family Foundation, and the S.D. Bechtel, Jr. Foundation. I'm grateful to each of them and to their officers for the encouragement and journalistic freedom they provided to me. Stephanie Banchero of the Joyce Foundation was the person who first approached me with the idea of delving more deeply into the question of noncognitive capacities and how they are developed. Katherine Bradley, the president of the CityBridge Foundation, offered me valuable direction and counsel when I had only the vaguest notion of what this project could be, and she continued to provide me with important insights and suggestions throughout the time I spent working on it. Her colleagues at CityBridge, including Amanda Nichols, Arthur McKee, Bethanie Glaser, and Mieka Wick, were also immensely helpful. Amanda guided me through the complex world of foundation support with wisdom and grace.

When I started working on this book, it wasn't a book; my original intention was for it to exist only as an online report. My literary agent, David McCormick, was the first person to conceive of it as a physical object, and he worked long and hard to shepherd it into existence. My editor at Houghton Mifflin

Harcourt, Deanne Urmy, along with Bruce Nichols and their colleagues, bent the rules of book publishing to enable us to publish and distribute this book in a variety of ways both old- and new-school. I am grateful to them for their collaboration and their support.

I feel exceptionally fortunate that Joel Lovell agreed to serve as my editor on this project. He is a gifted editor and a great friend, and his advice and guidance, editorial and otherwise, helped me through many obstacles. Pam Shime is an excellent researcher and fact-checker, as well as an all-around innovative thinker, and I benefited greatly from her insights into how to distribute this work in all of its incarnations. Similarly, I'm grateful to Dylan Greif for his keen design sense and also for his ability to think creatively about how to present this material in several different media at once. My thanks go also to Sean Cooper for his careful and clear-eyed copyediting, to Ann Clarke for her expert proofreading and last-minute editorial advice, and to Chelsea Cardinal for her beautiful cover design.

Mike Perigo volunteered his time and expertise as an adviser and sounding board from the earliest days of my reporting and writing. I benefited greatly from his careful reads of several drafts, as well as from the thoughtful comments of several other early readers, including David Yeager, Arthur McKee, Georgia Flight, Thomas Toch, Lija Farnham, Stephanie Banchero, Zoe Stemm-Calderon, and Anh Ton.

I'm grateful to the many researchers, scientists, and educators who took considerable time and great care to help me better understand their work and the work of others in their field, including David Yeager, Cybele Raver, Pamela Cantor, Sheila Walker, Philip Fisher, Mary Dozier, Clancy Blair, Jack Shonkoff, Camille Farrington, Kirabo Jackson, Ron Berger, Dacia Toll, and Jens Ludwig. I also want to thank the teachers, principals, and other practitioners who let me watch them work and then offered me their insights into why they do what they do, including Brett Kimmel, Margarita Prensa, Tara Goulet, Molly Brady, Ann Szekely, Jessica Sager, Janna Wagner, Brandon Bailys, Michelle Navarre, Roel Vivit, and John Wolf. I'm particularly grateful to Stephanie King for inviting me into her home and family and to the young men of the Becoming a Man group at Roberto Clemente Community Academy, who made me feel welcome and included in their discussion circle.

Much of this book was written at Left Hand Coffee in Montauk, New York, and I'm grateful to Danny, Dahiana, and Yannis for keeping their doors open and the tea and cortados flowing well after all the tourists had left town.

And finally, I am thankful to Ellington and Charles, who every day give me new insights into what growing up really means — how childhood can be simultaneously both an impossible challenge and an inexpressible delight. As always, my deepest gratitude goes to my wife, Paula, for showing me through her example that it is possible to transcend a childhood of adversity, even if that adversity never entirely leaves you behind, and for raising our two sons with the love and devotion that every child deserves.

A NOTE ON SOURCES

Detailed sources for the information in this book, along with graphs and charts illustrating many of the research studies described here, can be found in the online version of *Helping Children Succeed*, at paultough.com/helping.

ABOUT THE AUTHOR

Paul Tough is the author of three books, including this one. He is a contributing writer to *The New York Times Magazine* and a regular contributor to the public-radio program *This American Life*. His writing has also appeared in *The New Yorker*, *The Atlantic*, *GQ*, and *Esquire*. He has worked as an editor at *The New York Times Magazine* and *Harper's Magazine*, and as a producer for *This American Life*. He was the founding editor of *Open Letters*, an online magazine. He lives with his wife and two sons in Montauk, New York. For more information, please visit paultough.com, or follow Paul on Twitter: @paultough.

ABOUT THE TYPE

This book is set in Warnock Pro, a contemporary serif typeface designed by Robert Slimbach and released in 2000. It was created at the request of Chris Warnock for the personal use of his father, the Adobe co-founder and desktop-publishing pioneer John Warnock, after whom the typeface is named. Slimbach later expanded Warnock Pro into a multifaceted font family combining both classical and contemporary motifs and optimized for both modern printing and on-screen viewing.